With love

From

Don

May 11th 2010

Painting and Poetry
- *a new lease of life*

Don Brown

Published by Smileawhile-enterprise

15 Llanberis Grove, Nottingham, NG8 5DP

Published by Smileawhile-enterprise

First edition - published 2010

Edited by P. Lemard

Copyright © Don Brown 2010

All rights reserved

Whilst every effort has been made to fulfill requirements with regard to reproducing copyright material, the editor apologies for any omissions and will be glad to rectify any errors at the earliest opportunity.

A record of this book is available from the British Library

ISBN 978-0-9563030-3-5

Printed and bound in the UK by
Think Ink
11-13 Philip Road,
Ipswich, Suffolk, IP2 8BH

Smileawhile-enterprise
Nottingham

smileawhile-enterprise@hotmail.com

If I leave anything but happy memories, it is

bad planning.

INTRODUCTION	1
CHAPTER ONE	2
A Night To Remember	3
Father & Sons	11
Grandad Parkin	13
Grandad Brown	14
Dad	16
Uncles	18
CHAPTER TWO – LINKS WITH HISTORY	20
CHAPTER THREE – CHILDHOOLD REVISITED	28
Fairs & Wakes	29
Langley	32
A Schoolboy's Story – 1934	41
Memories Of Grandad	44
Blackpool	45
The Golden Mile	46
Judge Not	47
Don's Impression – One World	48
Wonderful World	49
Anagrams	51
The Evacuee	55
Observing	61
CHAPTER FOUR – MORE ADVENTURES	63
Football	64
Schoolboy Football	74
CHAPTER FIVE – FAMILY LIFE	81
Mum, Dad And Jean	82
Wedding Day 25 Dec 1919	83
New Season	87
Doctor's Appointment	89
Bridges	92
Canals	94

CHAPTER SIX – WORKING LIFE	**96**
CHAPTER SEVEN – LANDMARKS IN LIFE	**102**
The Eastwood Church Fire	103
Death Of A Loved One	108
Brown Eyes	110
Solitude	111
The Park	114
Blackpool Barbershop	117
CHAPTER EIGHT – THE AWAKENING	**119**
The Night That Changed It All	120
Party Time	121
July 1993	122
Painting And Poetry	123
CHAPTER NINE – A NEW LEASE OF LIFE	**127**
A Word From Don	129
What A Difference A Letter Makes	131
Sally	132
The Telephone	133
Messages	134
The dawing of the last day	135
Holy Trinity	136
Good Friday	137
Easter	138
Faith	141
Desiderata	144
Slavery	148
John Newton	150
Born To Be Hunted	155
Ramblings In Literature - My Favourite Authors	157
The Howitts	163
Fa Cup 2006	168
Burscough	172
Robert W. Service	174
Wanlockhead	177
Boxing	178

Stanley Park	185
Another Close Call	190
ASS U ME	191
I live to love	192
To my grandchildren – Rebecca & Julie	193
Don's Sayings	194

Introduction

I met up with Don Brown in September 2008, when he attended a concert at which I was singing.

Don has always been a source of encouragement to me and on this occasion, he was equally supportive. Bounding with energy and sporting his wonderful smile, I commented to Don that he seemed as though he had a new lease of life, as he beamed and jived around me like a young boy!

At that time aged 83, Don told me of how he had overcome depression and a brain haemorrhage and now felt so alive and refreshed. He proceeded to recite his poem entitled 'painting and poetry.'

I was so impressed and inspired by his life experiences that I asked him to post me a copy of his poem, which he insisted that I put to music for him. To my pleasure, Don kept his word, and on the following Monday, a selection of his writings arrived via the post; my favourites being, 'what a difference a letter makes' and 'I live to love.'

What a compelling story his life told! What a remarkable man!
A further meeting with this smiling man revealed his creative ability to produce sketches, paintings, exciting and amazing writings, so beautiful that I felt that they must be shared.
Paulet Lemard

Chapter One

A NIGHT TO REMEMBER

Friday 2nd July 1993 was a night I think I will remember for the rest of my life. I'd had a good day and night and retired to my bedroom about midnight. My life was changed completely.

I was doing voluntary work at the Eastwood Comprehensive School, giving of my knowledge, skills, experience and help to the staff and pupils there. Two years earlier I never believed I would enjoy life again, yet there I was, appearing to be enjoying life, but when I was alone, deep depressive moods hit and held me. Five days a week I was at school; seven nights a week I would go out drinking, conversing, singing, forgetting and getting away from reality. On Sundays I went to Church - I was and am a believer; knowing if I had not got my faith I would not be writing this.

So on the night of 2nd July 1993, it was dark and I had no idea of the time. I was awakened by a sharp, searing pain at the top left hand side of my head. I went downstairs. It felt as though something had burst in my head. I took two anadins, wrote down what had happened and what I had done. I unlocked my front door, put my phone on the floor, lay at the side of it and phoned the doctor. I got the answering machine, wrote down the number the machine gave me then proceeded to ring that number. A female voice answered me. I gave her my name and address and told her, "I'm going now." She asked, "Do you want an ambulance?" I said "I don't know what I want, I'm going." I put myself in the recovery position and 'went.'

I was aroused by two men speaking to me and putting me on to a stretcher. It was daylight. The sun was shining; my front door was open and a neighbour was standing at my gate. I remember nothing more until ten days later when I woke up.

  Petals of words, falling into my mind

 fanned by the gentle breeze of musical notes

   creating a beauty I cannot convey

     I am in Paradise

    in my own back garden

  If only I could show what my mind sees.

My son David said, "Dad I don't want to be last to know." I replied "I knew you could only sit and worry and do nothing to help me and I think they look after you when you live alone." David said, "I've got to agree." The neighbour, who was standing at the door when the ambulance arrived, rang him at 6.00am saying, "I don't want to alarm you but they're taking your dad away in the ambulance." David followed the ambulance and followed the stretcher with me on and says that as soon as I went through the door, a brain haemorrhage was diagnosed. He said that if he had stayed he felt they would be sending me back home so he left, returning two hours later.

I was in bed knowing nothing. Anyone who wanted could visit me. I had so many visitors that when I showed signs of improvement, they would only allow my closest friends and relatives to visit me. I had cards from hundreds of children along with dozens and dozens from friends and relatives also the Swimming club.

Who knows what occurred during those days and nights that Don lay unconscious in hospital?

Did he relive his life? Who knows?

One thing is certain, he did not emerge as his former self and his life would never be the same again.

As Don had to re-learn control of his limbs, he took to writing down his thoughts, drawing and painting pictures, which gave him inspiration from magazines, postcards and his own ideas.

The following writings, poems, thoughts and pictures are the jigsaw pieces that depict Don's recovery, and the memories he has had since his awakening and which have added to his new lease of life.

I was born on 20th August 1925, in a house called Olive Cottage, which was built by my grandfather, William Parkin and named after his youngest child, Olive. Grandad Parkin was a miner, having started down the pit when he was 11 years of age. He lived with his wife, Lucy. They had five sons and four daughters. For my delivery, my mother Lucy May Brown went to her parent's home, just as she had done for my brother's birth four years earlier on the 28th July 1921. He was named Frederick William after both Grandads; Frederick Ernest Brown being my paternal grandfather and William Parkin my maternal grandfather. I think my name may have been pulled out of the hat, yet I remember mum talking about a Scottish aunty so I will never know how or why I was called Donald.

We lived in an old farmhouse until I was about 8 years old. I have happy memories of that wonderful place, which has long since been pulled down - new buildings replacing the things I treasured. Six cottages, a terrace, adjoined the farmhouse. Originally they would have housed the farm labourers but for the first eight years of my existence I cannot recall any one leaving - we were the first family to go. I used to visit there quite often for my cousin Horace moved in and I liked him; he was good fun. He was married. They had no children and I remember he died while a young man.

That farmhouse must have been late 18th or early 19th Century for the walls were really thick. I often used to sit in the window at the bottom of the stairs next to the Staffordshire pot dog and looking down the yard at the row of houses that ran down from ours. We adjoined the terraces but we had outbuildings, all single storey except the first on the left hand side that adjoined the house, which had a loft reached by outside steps and a large back garden. There were no divisions between the cottages and the yards made a kind of drive finishing in a footpath, which led to a large house in which the Watsons resided. Running parallel to the cottages was a wall about two feet six inches tall with an opening to the garden of each cottage opposite each back door. The gardens were higher than the yards and steps were in every entrance. Halfway down the yards was the water pump that supplied us all I can remember turning the water taps on in the farmhouse but cannot recall the installation. The gardens were long and at the top of each were the toilets, ash pits and dustbins bounded by a hawthorn hedge. At the top of the farmhouse garden lay the fields.

The front garden was mostly lawns and flower beds with a lonely apple tree, it gave splendid eating apples called Molster - their only fault being they did not keep very well but that was no problem to me, I love apples they are my favourite fruit!

They were happy times but hard times; looking back, I would not change a thing if I could for I had love and fine examples set in front of me.

Next door down, were the Bailey's with their daughter, Joan. Joan was the same age as me but we did not get on very well. I think her Mum and Dad told Joan to keep away from that naughty boy next door. Grandad related one episode that sticks in my mind. Joan said, "I do not like Donald because hc swears." I replied with, "I don't like Joan. She dirties her knickers!"

Next-door down were the Davenports, an old couple with no children. Bill had worked for the council until his retirement. His first wife had died, and then he met Rose, who had never been married, but had been in service all her life as a wonderful cook and housekeeper. They were so different but appeared to be very contented. I used to run their errands but Mrs Davenport upset me by thinking that I was not responsible enough to go to 2 shops in one journey. A thing I always did when entering their house, was to go straight to the cupboard and shake the toffee tin. One night, Bill went out to a special event and he had a hard collar studded to his shirt. He came to our house to ask Dad to fasten it and when the event was over, he came round to our house late at night for Dad to take his collar off. How Mum and Dad laughed about that for a good while after.

Langley is a long village. Olive Cottage is at one end and the allotments at the other. Before I started going to school, grandad and I would set off for the allotments. He would put me in his barrow and wheel me all the way there. When I started school, after 1930, it was just during school holidays. A lovely big shed stood at the top of the garden. There was a seat at the back. The top opened and all the tools were stored inside.

The main London Midland and Scottish Railway line from London to Scotland ran by the side of the garden. Grandad made me a double peg signal and I was in charge of all the trains that passed through; 1 peg for goods and 2 pegs for expresses. I got to know the names of the engines and the trains at an early age. Some of them are with me now, e.g. The Windward Isles pulling the Waverley comes to mind. The garden had a shed, a toilet, a wash basin; windows on one side and front, but best of all signals, that grandad had made for me to be in charge of all the trains that came through the L.M.S. main railway line. Puffing Billy, the engine that served the mines, would not take any notice he always did just what he wanted to.

Father & Sons

Don, James, Fred

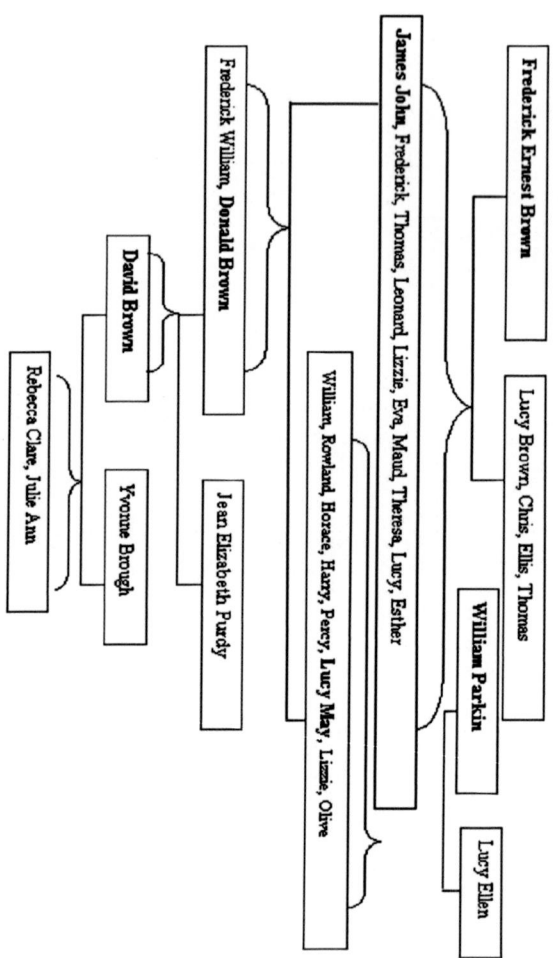

GRANDAD PARKIN

Grandad would work steadily all day. He was a good gardener. His allotment was the means of feeding the family; his garden behind Olive Cottage, a delight to the eye and a delight to be in, with it's little winding paths, greenhouse, summerhouse, ornaments and flowerbeds.

Grandad never went to school. He started work down New Eastwood pit when he was 11 years old. Before that he had worked in the fields. He told me tales of himself cutting the grass and of his ponies down the pit - his favourite pony was called Smiler. He often sat me on his knee, telling me stories and singing me folk songs. He taught me to tell the time; he cut my hair. He could not read or write. Grandma would read to him and she had taught him to sign his name. He had never been to school. His pleasures were listening to the news and when that was on no one must speak; he smoked a pipe and he went to the Butchers Arms some evenings and had halves of mild ale. Often when I was on his knee he would peel an apple; the peel coming off in one continuous string then the succulent juicy fruit cut in to thin slices. Sheer delight in simple pleasures!

GRANDAD BROWN

Grandad Brown was named Frederick Ernest. He too was a good gardener. He lived in Langley Mill with Grandma. Grandad was a deputy in the coal mining industry. Grandma was in service at Brook Farm, Loscoe. She was 17 years of age when she married Grandad. My father was the eldest child of the marriage, born on the 3rd of November 1898. There were 4 sons James John, Frederick, Thomas and Leonard along with 6 daughters namely Elizabeth always known as Lizzie, Eva, Maud Theresa Lucy and Esther. I knew them all except Esther, who met an early death by falling down the stairs of the house in Bridge Street, Langley Mill. My grandparents on dad's side, Frederick Ernest and Lucy Ellen Esther, who lived in Bridge Street, Langley Mill, moved from Codnor, Derbyshire after James John, my father, was born. On my grandparent's marriage certificate of 1896, my great grandfather's fathers name is given as Thomas Ward (Deceased). Through things I have heard I assume that on the death of my paternal great grandfather, the said Frederick Ernest, my grandfather was reared and cared for by my grandmother's parents.

Grandad became the night watchman at the G.R. Turner factory. G.R. Turner Ltd, an engineering firm of Langley Mill established in 1874, ceased to be in 1980. In the 1950's wages were paid on Friday nights at a window in the General Office. With the banks being closed on Good Friday, the Bank Roll was delivered on Maundy Thursday, at 5.00pm on that evening. Grandad was on duty, locked in the office with his dog, (always a black Cocker Spaniel) food and his double-barrelled shotgun until relieved by the office staff at 9.00am on Good Friday morning. His front room was his den. He had guns on 3 walls and more in a rack. The guns on the wall were double-barrelled shotguns. His others included a single-barrel folding gun and a stick gun. He prized them both highly and was proud of them. His chest of drawers stood in the corner and held his ammunition, which included cartridges, wads, powder, shot etc. Grandad taught me to fill the cartridges and how to handle the guns, stressing the safety precautions, but he never took me shooting; Uncle Tom did. All the farmers in the district gave Grandad access to their land and the stew pot was never empty. Grandad also made my first fishing rod, making the top section with split cane and took me fishing. I never became a good angler – that was not grandad's fault!

He was a very clever man; in the 1930's, he devised permutations on the Football coupons. He taught me many things with figures that I still remember.

DAD

Dad was the eldest child. He was born in Codnor and was christened James John Brown. He told me that when he was a small boy he walked to Woodlinkin farm to collect skimmed milk free of charge before returning home with it, then heading off to school. Dad must have done well at school for he went straight into a job in the offices of G.R. Turner Ltd. At the age of 16 years, he was elected as the secretary of Langley Mill United Cricket Club, where he remained until the outbreak of the 1st World War. My brother Frederick and I each have the 2 medals, which Dad received during his service at the club. He was instrumental in bringing Billy Voce, the Notts County cricketer to Langley Mill. Bill was then 15 or 16 years old. I hold Langley Mill Cricket Club very dear as I do Heanor Town Cricket Club. I was divided between the 2. I've seen great matches on both grounds during the late 1920's, 1930's and early 1940's.

I never heard anything of grandad's relations but heard much of grandma's 4 brothers; Christopher whom I knew, Ellis who fought a bear at Ripley Fair, Thomas who was drowned in the canal basin and Henry. Henry was a bare fist fighter. In those days it was common to give anyone in the fighting game named Henry, the nickname of Chicken, so he was known as Chicken Brown. Chris was a good runner and told me how he won a road race from Codnor Market Place to the Eclipse Inn, Loscoe and then celebrated in the Eclipse with his brothers.

He was a powerful man with immense strength, well built and of fine physique. I knew him well, and he lived with Grandad and Grandma until his death. Great-uncle Chris was a face worker down the mine. The reason for him leaving his work at the pit was caused by a fall of coal, his arm being pinned to the ground by the fall. With his own strength he released himself dislocating his shoulder in the process. Ever after he had great difficulty putting on his overcoat but he would not let himself be beaten by anything. He got extra money to his pension by wheeling in loads of coal delivered to the local miners. In those days a load of coal was part payment of wages by the coalmine owners and being well liked, Chris got plenty of work. He always dined alone - he didn't mind me being there when I was small, and as I grew I dropped the watching off. I have never seen a man have such big dinners as Chris had or anyone shift coal with such speed! He was fast on his feet too. Grandma was in service at Brook Farm, Loscoe before she married Grandad. She told me that during that period Chris had won a road race from Codnor to the Eclipse Inn, Loscoe. Chris also told me how his feet saved him. Chris and some of his mates had gone behind the mill in to Mill Fields to have a game of cards. They were playing nap. Somebody had just bid 3 when a voice came from behind the hedge, "NAP, and I've got the lot!" It was the village bobby. Time for action!! Great-uncle Chris was saved by his speedy legs!

Grandma was a wonderful cook, when I started my apprenticeship with G.R. Turner I saw much more of her and Grandad. Grandad became the night watchman at the G.R. Turner factory and when he died I went to Grandmas and helped in any way I could. Eventually she could not manage on her own and lived with my mum and dad for a while, my wife got to know grandma well. They had great admiration for each other. Jean loved grandma and she was the first grandparent she had known. On every visit Jean would take Grandma a present and Grandma would give Jean a hug.

Uncles

The communal back yard was where uncle Len, had a pigeon loft. When he got married and left home, he and Uncle Tom kept the loft going for a good while. Uncle Fred lived in the next street. He had pigeons too. My dad was the only son not to have pigeons and Grandad never appeared to bother with pigeons either.

My uncle Len was a toolmaker. All his working life was spent at G.R. Turner, broken only by a spell in the Royal Engineers during the Second World War, during that time he was working on Mulberry Harbours. Uncle Fred and Uncle Tom spent all their working lives at G.R. Turner, mainly on the drilling machines. They both could grind drills by hand to cut perfectly round holes to the exact size of the drill. Great skill is needed for this - I was lucky to have such expert tutors.

Chapter Two

Links with History

David Herbert Lawrence was born, the fourth of five children in 1885 at Eastwood, Nottinghamshire. In a poem he wrote 'my father was a working man ... my mother was a superior soul... .'

He attended Nottingham High School and Nottingham University College and wrote over 1200 poems. Many think his poetry a bi product but I consider that it contains his finest work. In one of his letters he writes, 'I have always tried to get an emotion out in its own course, without altering it. I don't write for your ear. I can't tell you what pattern I see in any poetry, save one complete thing.' After his death Frieda wrote, 'What he had seen and felt and known he gave in his writing to his fellow men, the splendour of living, the hope of more and more life a heroic and immeasurable gift... .'

In spite of what many people think, I think that the incentive for Lawrence's writing was love for his fellow men. Not a sentimental, squelchy, superficial love but a dry, hard one to make people sit up and tackle their job of living. Lawrence tried to get beyond the very core of moral judgment, material consideration, abuse and convention. From his genuine own experience he knew that one of the stumbling blocks to a more complete life was sex and desire. The power and glory of sex, the desire of men and women for each other, the very root of our being had become a shameful and hidden thing. I recall that as child, the legs of grandma's tables were covered, to prevent scratches and damage I thought, but actually it was the unspoken way of those times which said, no legs were to be shown in that house. If today, all desire for women from men, along with the desire for men from women should stop, in not so many years human beings would vanish from the face of the earth! So Lawrence wrote about sex, he opened the door. Harry T Moore writes in his book, 'The Priest of Love,' as a frail, shy boy that when he saw people, landscapes and animals, they struck upon his sensitivity more sharply than upon the sensitivities of others. He was then only receiving, as a quiet child, the hints of what he would one day transmit so forcefully.

Lawrence's early experiences with pet animals were in many cases sad, to say the least. His mother never wanted animals in the house. To her the animal world, like that of the miners, was dirty. On two occasions Mrs Lawrence gave way. Lawrence wrote two sketches; Adolph and Rex. Adolph was a rabbit; Rex a puppy. The sketches gave lively portraits of both animal and family life; the love of the children, the father always a friend, mother always regretting she had given way. Lawrence eventually wrote stories and poems of many different animals. I have not yet found a poet who can get the insight or nearness to nature, the same as Lawrence.

John Lawrence, D. H. Lawrence's grandfather, was brought up in Nottingham, maybe born there. He moved to Brinsley in the 1850's. He was a tailor supplying the miners with their pit clothes. Lawrence's sister Ada, a friend of my mother in law, Ida Walker Calladine who was a descendant of the Walker of Barber and Walker, described him more highly as one who made gentlemens' clothing.

Arthur Lawrence married Lydia Beardsall on 27th December 1875 in St Stephen's Parish Church, Sneinton. Firstly they lived in Sutton in Ashfield, then in Old Radford, then to Brinsley and so to Victoria Street, Eastwood. When D.H Lawrence was two years old, the family moved down to the Breach, Eastwood. When he was six they moved to Walker Street, where he lived until he was 18 years old. in one of his letters he wrote, 'Go to Walker Street, stand in front of the third house, look across at Chrich on the left, Underwood in front, High Park woods and Annesley on the right; I know that view better than any in the world.'

Lawrence last visited Eastwood, in 1926 for the Wakes. He mentioned the wakes in Sons and Lovers. I have found mention of Teddy Raynor's travelling theatrical troupe, who are referred to in his letters, and this brings me to another connection.

I have a map of Langley Mill (c. 1900) showing a Picture Theatre where my father, Jas. J. Brown was in charge of projecting the films and the stage shows presented there. He told me many tales of that place and the plays performed by Teddy Raynor and his troupe, including Maria Martin, Murder in the Red Barn, Sweeny Todd, the Demon Barber, even Shakespeare and Dickens. D. H. Lawrence also mentions the Eastwood Statutes Fair in his short story, 'Tickets Please.' The Statutes Fair was held in November. My Grandad Parkin told me it was just off the Nottingham Road at the west end of Eastwood in the first field before the Sun Inn. He met my grandma there. She was born in Beggarlee, Eastwood in 1862. Grandad was born in Langley, Heanor in 1861. The Rev. (Baron) Von Hube officiated their wedding in Greasley Church on 18th April 1881.

The Statutes Fair was a gathering of people some who wanted to be hired and some who wanted to hire, the rest spectators. A contract was for a year; the bond sealed by the handing over of a penny by the hirer to the hired. Grandma was in service as a maid (housekeeper, dogsbody, you name it). Grandad was not for hire because he started work at New Eastwood pit in 1871. They went on to celebrate their Diamond Wedding; they had eleven children, the sons being William, Rowland, Horace, Harry and Percy a twin the other twin being stillborn. The daughters were Eliza, Lucy May (my mother), Lizzie and Olive.

The East Window of Eastwood Church 1950

Chapter Three

Childhood Revisited

FAIRS & WAKES

My first recollection of a fair as a youngster was when I was taken to Heanor Fair in November 1930.

Grandad Parkin was a retired miner and before I started school, I spent much time with him. Heanor Fair was held on the market square, with stalls down the two adjoining streets namely Wilmot Street and Abbott Street.

The big steam engines generated all the electricity needed for the whole show. The biggest ride was the Dragons. The rides that I remember from that time are the caterpillar, cakewalk, swing boats and the galloping horses complete with steam organ.

The stalls I recall were the coconut shy, a man making toffee, roll a penny and the tank roll. I liked the tank roll, along with the toffee man. The tanks were about 4 inch long and 1½ inch rounded end enclosing a ball bearing, all beautifully made, soldered and polished. I remember them to this day. I became an engineer and whenever I was soldering, I always thought of that work and tried to equal it.

The smells, the steam engines, the gleaming brass work, the engineers and the hard work to keep everything working and road worthy! Wonderful!

Later I went to see the Fairs and Wakes with my mates so my mind wanders to Hilltop Wakes, Eastwood, held in two fields. A feature of the Wakes was a Christian service held on the grounds on the first Sunday in September, referred to as Wakes Sunday.

Walking home from the Wakes one Saturday night at the junction of Nottingham Road and Mansfield Road, a moth hit the centre light. The lights were suspended from the trolley bus line columns that ran from Ripley to Nottingham, the longest trolley bus route in the United Kingdom at that time. The moth fell to the ground, stunned. I had won a bowl at the Wakes. I put the moth in the bowl, covered it with my hanky and took it home. The moth had a wingspan of 4 to 5 inches!
The next day, Dad took it to Dr Jacks, who knew about moths. He identified it as a Privet Hawk moth and kept it. I never knew what he did with it.

My great-uncle Chris was a good athlete. He won a road race from Codnor market place to the Eclipse inn at Loscoe. He was the only great-uncle that I knew and told me the following story. Ilkeston Fair was always noted for its Boxing Booth, run by brothers; (Woods, I think they were called). Chris, Henry (Chicken) a bare fist fighter, Thomas and Ellis were at Ripley Fair, at the turn of the 20th Century. The three brothers set Ellis up to fight a bear for prize money. The battle took place in the market square. Ellis went straight out and hit the bear on the nose. He was doing alright until the owner called out, "Get him, Grizzle" and the bear set about Ellis and had to be pulled off him!

LANGLEY

Just outside the small town of Heanor in Derbyshire lies the village of Langley. It once had a workhouse, a tan yard, a church mission, a mine, two chapels, three farms, three pubs, two Cooperative stores, a beer off, two general local grocery stores, three sweet shops, a cobblers shop, a swimming pool, a chip shop, a castle and a school that was for the infants and the senior girls of Langley and Marpool. Some village!

Hands Road (past)

As I write I can see the place I knew in the 1920's. On my last visit I stood and photographed the places I remembered. One of these places has not altered much, for in 2002 I painted my first landscape, taken from a small black and white snapshot; the only difference being the old gas street lamp having gone, and a pavement being put alongside the road. Yes, there were gas light street lamps, lit by the lamplighter Mr Hutchinson. We had a knocker up also, maybe the same man.

Hands Road (present)

The workhouse was a large stone building. It was a residence for families, I played around it but never did enter, and the church mission was next door; both buildings long since gone. The tan yard was next to the pit. The mine was in production, the tan yard was not. It's buildings housed families, we called these tan yard row.

The two chapels were the Primitive Methodist and the White Chapel. My parents were members of the Primitive Methodists. I was invited to the celebration of the chapel's centenary; I went along and enjoyed the meeting with old friends. That chapel is no more but the white one still stands.

The three farms were Billy Holmes, Wardles and the Lacey Fields Farm. Lacey Fields farm is the only one surviving as a farm. It no longer belongs to the Cooperative society. In the old days a gala was held there every year. I often won the groceries for the week at those galas, for I was quite a good runner then. That was the village I was born in.

The three pubs were The Colliers Rest, The Old Arab and The Butchers Arms. The first to go was the Old Arab then The Colliers Rest so Langley manages with one pub - the one which the old Langley Rovers had their meetings in, changed in for their home matches before that trek to Langley Mill, then win, lose or draw, celebrate in on Saturday nights. They were the first football team I supported. I played with them on the recreation ground. We had a goalpost at one end of the pitch, piles of coats at the other. The swimming pool, actually two pools, one was four foot deep at one end and two foot deep at the other. The other went from six foot to four foot and had a high board and a springboard at the deep end. Trees overhung the deepest pool. Mr Boam was in charge. He was responsible for the cleaning and heating, making sure we had a cold shower and were clean and respectable; he also collected the money.

I joined the Cooperative Youth Club, the youth club was mixed sex. My father was a member of the local cooperative society committee and was instrumental in bringing the youth club into being. We had a football team and an athletic squad along with many more activities, it was a good club.

The castle, which was not a castle - a Mr Newton decided that his cottage was in such a prominent position he would make it a landmark for posterity, he started to extend upwards. He had gone up quite a good way when the local council intervened making him pull some down. It finished three floors high, a bungalow-like extension was added which stood out over the hilltop; a row of houses flanked it on it's opposite side. The local people gave it the name of Langley Castle.

Langley Chapel

My thoughts are of pleasure when I think of Langley – the village of my birth in the heart of the Nottinghamshire and Derbyshire Coalfield. I thank God each day for my parents, my brother and my grandparents; for the love they gave me and the sacrifices they made for me.

I recall the centenary of the church, which started me and gave me the base to build on. I can see the faces of the stalwarts of the church when I was a boy. The people I look back on, who gave me examples by which I set my standards. I thank God for them all.

A village, in the time of my boyhood was a terrific community, where friendship abounded and help was always given when needed. As a boy, events in the village stood out and many were associated with the chapel anniversary, social treats, concerts and outings. Sacrifices were made so that everyone had an enjoyable time.

Across the road from the Church lived Mr Charlie Flint. My grandmother was midwife and present at Mr Flint's birth. Mr Flint presided at grandma's funeral and saw her out - such was the closeness of village life.

As a boy, who was always fed and always clothed, I did not realise what hardship abounded and what efforts were made. Looking back, I know and now realise what wonderful people made up my village! I see them all, place them and know that I was so lucky to be born in Langley, to benefit from what they were doing and to have the family life that I was given.

The village was not without character; the drunks, the rogues, the adulterers but most of all we had our family circles. I am confident that if we had the same strength of family circles today, our problems would not be so great.

The first school that I attended was Langley Infants. It was a united school, being used by senior girls of Langley and Marpool. Miss Nunne was the senior teacher of the Infants school and Miss Barfoot was the Headmistress. The building is still standing and still being used as a school. My mother attended there. I have or had a group photo of mother and her schoolmates. I also have a photo of me as a 5 year old, dancing round the Maypole, 30 years later. (That's me, second in on the right, just in front of the girl in the white dress.)

In winter, we had big open fires with heavy iron guards. The colliery was across the road. I don't know if we got the coal from there but we sure did burn some. There were no pithead baths and we saw the colliers in their work clothes with their black faces and hands at the end of the shift. What a job! What an existence for a pittance. My Grandad started on the pit face when he was 11 years old. Children of today say they are bored – he was too tired to be bored! I don't want those times back but I have to ask if we have made life easier for the fit and healthy.

After 5 years, I moved up to Marpool Boys School. Mr Hollingsworth (Fesky) was Headmaster and he had his allotment about 50 yards from the school. He would get lads to go and work in it. He had hives there too; no wonder he'd got one of the best gardens in the district! He was a strict man. He caught Jim Millward and me shooting water pistols. He gave us 6 of the best. Jim kept pulling his hand back. Fesky came back up sharp so Jim got an extra one on his knuckles for luck. That was Fesky!

Miss Henson (Fanny) took Standard 2. She was ok but lost her temper very quickly. She could bite the big red and blue marking pencils in half with one snap! If you noticed her cheek muscles moving, you'd watch out; something was going to happen but no one knew what, not even Fanny. Something was going to fly; someone would be clouted; pencil to be bitten; no one knew – SURPRISE! Miss Pearson took the next class. She was firm, patient and constant, a model of the qualities a teacher should have, but Fanny was exciting.

A SCHOOLBOY'S STORY – 1934

Today is very warm. We'll go fishing and dangle our feet in the brook. When we've had enough we'll stand in the water, hang on to Rover – that's my dog. We know a good spot where it is shallow. Tom is small but he can stand up and he's very clever. Tom is frightened and his Dad will kill him if he gets drowned. His Dad told him. His Dad is big; he goes down the pit. He's got a big moustache; he goes to the pub; he shouts at us. I don't like his Dad but I like Tom. He tells me lots of things. He's very clever.

Jim can swim. I like Jim but I think he's a liar. He told me he saw God the other day. Nobody's seen God, my Dad told me. Jim's Dad gives me fag cards and he gives Jim a ha'penny to get some sweets – he's got to give us one, his Dad told him. We'll all bite 'em and give Rover a bit. Rover likes us all. Tom says there are 480 ha'pennies in a pound – that's a lot of sweets. Tom's very clever.

We play fag cards after school and at playtime, skimming on and knocking down – doubles for knocking down. We play marbles as well. We make sure to finish well before the bell rings for the end of play time 'cos everybody dives in to get the fag cards and marbles off the floor.

Fesky teaches us at school. He takes us to his allotment over the road from the school and we dig. He's got beehives as well. He canes us if we do something he doesn't like. He's got the best allotment in the land; Jim's Dad says so.

It stinks where we fish. The brook goes into the tan-yard just after the spot where we fish. It's the tan-yard that stinks. We have sticks, black cotton, matchsticks and worms. We catch sticklebacks and a few redbreasts. After fishing and wading we lie on the bank in the sun. Rover lies with us. We pretend to throw and Rover chases. Then he comes back and lies down and looks in my eyes. His eyes are brown, like cough drops taken out of my mouth to see if they've got smaller.

Tom's sister's having a baby. Mary, the maid at the farm told me. She tells me lots. She told me about babies. She is my friend. George, the cowman, was having a drink with Mary and pushing up to her. She said, "You ought to have more sense with the boy about." He went into the fields and I walked through the garden with Mary. I gathered flowers and gave them to her. She kissed me on the lips. I love Mary and I'm going to marry her if she saves herself for me. I'm nine now.

Memories of Grandad

We would walk along the prom and now the pier. Grandad told me when and how it was built. As I sat on his knee, he sang to me and we ate an apple. He would peel it all in one long slice; the peel would never break! And now I sit and look at the Tower – the one he saw. I now can see what tales he would tell me - the 'beggar's ramble' and much, much more. As I sat on his knee over seventy years ago, I recall those yellow badges along the mantelpiece - badges of the tower and the wheel. All that remains of the wheel is the blue plaque to mark the place where it stood.

BLACKPOOL

The sun is shining bright;
a soft breeze gently blows.
Morning's here; gone's the night.
People strolling; dogs a' pulling
Women gazing, their men tutting;
now and then a cackle, then a titter
Young men running, getting fitter;
come tonight on the bitter.

Plane flying overhead. Kids dragging feet of lead;
wishing other things instead.
Time goes by no matter what
Charity collector puts you on the spot,
makes you thankful for what you've got.
Many to that tin are giving;
those who do, glad of living.

More and more people pass,
another short-skirted lass
What they're thinking no one knows.
All aspects passing by,
even in the lovely sky, the tower above scanning all;
Down below we pass and meet,
pigeons gather round our feet; folks toss stuff to eat
More and more a real hub hub.
Now they're gone. So's the grub!

THE GOLDEN MILE

Pop by the gallon
Ice cream by the ton,
All being shifted, just for fun.
At the seaside everything goes;
where the money's gone, no one knows.
Happiness, laughter, many a tear
Everything happens – same every year!
Still we keep coming
so well we might
just to join in,
just for the sight.
Worries forgotten except for a few
Plenty to see: plenty to do.
Hustle and bustle, pushed with the crowd
plenty of colour; everything loud
Raindrops fall; life changed in a flash
Now the slot machines are taking the cash.

JUDGE NOT

He squats on the ground

A card in his hand, tired and homeless

Instead of young and healthy

Who knows? Maybe wealthy -

Jag parked round the corner

Nip back home, have a sauna.

He's got time to spare

Just to sit and stare

He moves his head slowly

He's been trained

His eyes are sharp, always craned

His hands are soft, no hard graft.

Facial features full of craft

What a way. What's he thinking?

I don't know. I turn away

but am I right? I'm not helping!

Don's impression – One World

WONDERFUL WORLD

A kid's world – a wonderful place
Goes with that beautiful face.
They see it all and know
We cannot follow: they need to go.
When they are happy,
getting love and care,
it shows and shows,
out it flows
A marvellous place, full of delight
Morning, evening, noon and night.
We stand, wonder – still can't find
What's inside that young mind.
Sometimes puzzled, with a frown
Then, laughter, glee, fancy free,
running, following that bouncing ball,
jumping, tumbling then the fall
I'm happy to stand, watch and see
Knowing once, that was me!

When I moved up to Heanor Grammar School, it was called Secondary School. I stayed there until the outbreak of war in 1939. I was not a great academic. I loved physics and I loved mathematics. I enjoyed school and spent many hours of sport and played for my house, Flamstead, at football. My first form teacher was Ma Dawson. She was lovely – not pretty or beautiful but lovely in all aspects. She made us all love her – it just happened. We boys played horrible boyish tricks on her but she took them in her stride. She never appeared to be upset or made us feel sorry for our actions, with her calmness and serenity. I feel that we loved her more each day; I know I did.

My next form tutor, until I left school on the outbreak of war, was Mr Sears (Tumby). He was the Geography master. I was not bad at Geography and I enjoyed it so we had a reasonable relationship. I was never given a detention or the cane so I must have got away with quite a bit!

ANAGRAMS

Margaret Thatcher	That great charmer
The Morse Code	Here come dots
Eleven plus two	Twelve plus one
Mother in Law	Woman Hitler
Dormitory	Dirty Room
Desperation	A Rope Ends It
Evangelist	Evils Agent
Slot Machines	Cash lost in em!
Alec Guinness	Genuine Class
Semolina	Is no meal
The Earthquakes	That queer shake
Telegraphs	Great helps
Sweetheart	There we sat
Astronomers	No more stars
Time	Emit

Catalogues	Got as a clue
Elegant	Neat leg
Sir Robert Peel	Terrible Poser
Old England	Golden Land
Parishioners	I Hire Parsons
Radical Reform	Rare mad frolic
Immediately	My ideal time
Midshipman	Mind his Map
Revolution	To love ruin
Presbyterians	Best in prayers
Matrimony	Into my arm
Masquerade	Queer as mad
Parliament	Partial men
Horatio Nelson	The Noon Sailor
Funeral	Real fun

The shortest writing I have read containing nearly all the letters of the alphabet is...

Pack my bag with five-dozen liquor jugs. Only six over, can you do any better?

THE EVACUEE

It was just after his fourth birthday that Raymond Frost stood on the platform of Birmingham railway station hand in hand with his twin brother Kenneth. He did not know what was happening or where they were being taken. The year was 1940; they evacuees, being taken to a safer place than the much bombed and to be bombed Birmingham. Hundreds and hundreds of boys and girls, each with a gas mask over their shoulder and a name label round their neck were shepherded into the coaches of the waiting train, then whisked away to Derby. There, buses were waiting to take them to various villages of Nottinghamshire and Derbyshire. Raymond and his brother were on one of the buses bound for Langley Mill.

Arriving at Langley Mill they got off the bus at the bottom of Bridge Street on the ground known as Parliament Square. Local people had gathered to greet them and choose whom they would take back to their homes, to house, rear and give family life to. Raymond and Kenneth waited and waited. Raymond said, "I don't think anyone wants us." Kenneth, who was a very highly-strung lad, threw a tantrum. He was transported to Dunstead House, the depot for evacuees who had not found homes. He remained there for the duration of the war.

Raymond was found a home but he didn't stay long in that place, so it was off to Dunstead House for him as well. Raymond vividly remembers the man who was in charge of the depot for he always carried a stick and needed neither excuse nor reason for using it; he was always hitting the children. Raymond thinks he got more than his fair share of those beatings. They were not happy memories of Dunstead House, but the children had to stick together; whatever happened for the worse it was always the evacuees who had been the cause.

It was the same at school; the local children picking on the evacuees, always blaming them for the damage or anything that could be thought of, to land them in trouble.

The first school that Raymond went to was the Nursery on the corner of Gladstone Street and Cromford Road, then to Aldercar Infants and finally to Langley Mill Boys. He was a quiet boy. One day the school bully decided to pick on him, Raymond stood his ground. A fight followed, all the lads encircling and cheering on the contestants of that battle, Raymond came out the victor. He was an instant hero - bullying had finished. He was wiping himself down and tidying himself up when he heard a voice "Come with me. I want a word with you." Raymond thought, 'I'm in for it now!' It was Stingy

Nettley, a very strict teacher. How wrong Raymond was! Stingy said, "You've done very well, I'm very pleased with you. You've taken a lot and have now done what was needed. Well done boy." Raymond could have hugged Stingy and has loved him ever since.

After another spell in Dunstead House, Raymond was found another home in Queen Street. The thing he remembers most about that place was Sunday afternoons, when he was put to a table with a large Bible and told to read. He was not a very good reader at this time, so he just looked at the pictures, he doesn't know how long he sat at these sessions but knows it seemed to be ages and ages. While he was reading he was given his only treat - it was his weekly treat. He was given a glass of raspberry vinegar diluted with water. He didn't last long at this home; an accident of nature was the cause of his early departure. So it was back to Dunstead House. The only consolation this brought was being reunited with Kenneth. This was the last spell at the depot for Raymond; he was found another home in Queen Street. He fitted in and straightway, he called the man of the house, dad and his wife, mam. He was with these people for the rest of the war. He was happy and he was loved. The couple had a son who was away at the war and Raymond helped to fill this gap.

Mam dished out any discipline. Dad never hit Raymond but he taught him a lesson and he has never neglected anything since that lesson. It was at the time most lads had rabbits and Raymond had rabbits. Dad said, "It's time you cleaned them rabbits out. If you don't clean them out, they are going." Raymond didn't clean them out. One day he came home from school, the rabbits were hanging up ready for the pot. He cried. Later at dinner he didn't eat, he just sat and regretted. Dad said, "I told you they would go." Dad taught Raymond gardening and he enjoys gardening to this day. As a young boy Raymond loved nature, going for walks with his mates, going fishing, finding bird nests, returning to them, finding the eggs hatched, eventually the young fledged the nest; then along the canal bank, looking for water voles, water hens, crayfish, bulrushes and barges being loaded with coal at the wharf - all happy times and wonderful memories.

One day he found a magpie, lying under the tree it had fallen out of. He took it home and reared it but eventually it brought him trouble. The lady next door had hung her washing out. It had been raining leaving the path and garden wet and dirty. Maggie had gone down the line pulling out all the pegs leaving washing strewn all over the path and garden.

On another occasion he stole one of dad's fags - it was one dad was smoking! He had just put it down when Maggie swooped and took it. He'd got to go! Raymond carried him to Cocker House Lane, with wet eyes and leaden heart. He said his last goodbyes and released him. Raymond ran all the way back to Queen Street but Maggie beat him, there he was shouting to him as he got to the back yard. Raymond still fed him but did not play or take him with him, after that and Maggie went out of his life.

He spent more and more time walking. On one of these walks round Codnor Castle and Stoneyford he saw a grass snake. He picked it up and put it in his pocket. On getting home he hung his coat up. Mam always checked his pockets for hankies etc. Imagine the shock on finding a snake! He was given a smack and told to get rid of the snake. He did that.

The war ended. Raymond did not want to go back to Birmingham, but he was sent back. He wrote a letter stating he did not want to be back in Birmingham and posted it, but not having put a stamp on the envelope, it arrived back at his Birmingham home. His real father confronted him saying, "I'm ashamed of you but if you want to go back you can!" Raymond didn't like the dirty city; he loved the nature and the life he had found.

When he got back to his Birmingham home with seven children and mam and dad, all the children had a bath, in a small tin bath, next day mam made a rice pudding in that same bath, the place was a slum.

Arrangements were made he came back to Langley Mill and was adopted by the couple he had stayed with. On leaving school he started work in the mines. When he was twenty he joined the Coldstream Guards and served with the Guards for two and a half years. On demobilization he married a local girl and settled down in Langley Mill. Later they moved to Eastwood where they still reside. They have a son and a daughter, along with three grandchildren. Raymond Frost does not walk the streets of Eastwood for he carries the name of that wonderful couple, who took him to their hearts.

OBSERVING

Looking out of the staff room window
all kinds of life I see
Those who start the rumpus,
step back now it's begun,
Those who cheer the losing one,
to see more, watch their fun.
Leaders, followers, cheerers, stallers
What will they be?
This or that,
who knows?
Maybe, just grow old.

Chapter Four

More Adventures

FOOTBALL

I played my first football match on a correctly marked out pitch, with real goalposts and nets in September 1936. I had just started the Heanor Grammar School, with my elder brother having been there before me, I had joined in games on the local recreation ground with him and his pals, so I was known. I was selected to play for the Flamstead House. There being three Houses in the school, Flamstead, Howitt and Ray.
- Flamstead, after the 1st Astronomer Royal born in Denby, Derbyshire.
- Howitt, after William and Mary Howitt, both writers of renown. William was born in Heanor, Mary in Uttoxeter.
- Ray, after a noted Heanor family.

At the football match, Don Beighton, a large ginger haired lad, either a 5th or 6th former, was in goal for the Ray team. I remember running towards him with the ball at my feet. He ran towards me, arms waving, face contorted, shouting and doing his best to put me off. Me, a small insignificant 1st year student, I beat him like I had done the lads on the recreation ground. I feinted to the left, put him on his wrong foot and slipped the ball to Doug Williamson, one of the lads in the same year as my brother. He scored; we won!

G.R. Turners Football Team

Back Row: John Chambers, Les Rodgers, Jonah Longden, Cyril Charlton, Clem Clifton
Front Row: Gordon Clay, Don Brown, Dennis Harper, Pete Sisson, Norman Wade, Hamer Brown.

On leaving school in 1939, I signed as an engineering apprentice with G.R. Turner Limited, and continued my education at the Heanor Mining and Technical College. My next football team was Langley Mill Coop Youth Club. My dad was on the Langley Mill and Aldercar Cooperative Society committee. He had no dealings with the running of the Youth Club but his committee provided the cash to help keep the football team running. The youth club was for both sexes, very successful, same as the football team. Many of the lasses travelled along with us to our matches. Travelling was always on public transport, unless by foot. We played our home matches on the ground behind what is now the Trent Bus Garage at Langley Mill on Aldreds Lane; a railway bridge overlooks it.

That was when Mum and Dad had come to watch the match in which Hamer Brown received a blow. We gave him the cold-water treatment dragged him to the side, then got back to the game. I don't think they came to see me again while I was playing for that team! Two happy seasons!

Then to Loscoe, Daddy Groome, unsung hero! Daddy could not have been bettered. When a young one thinks old men have always been old; that was how I was with Daddy. I don't know what position he held in the Church, I didn't ask. Daddy just got to me with his- football, big hands, big hat, big coat and big heart. I see him carrying that football now. I don't know how I joined up with Loscoe, but I did and made many friends. So I progressed to the Derby Senior League with Loscoe Miners Welfare, run by another stalwart Joe Wesson. I remember some of the players and I certainly remember the grounds and the receptions we got especially if we had beaten their teams. The players Dennis and Reg Hardy, George Nichols, Hector Webster, George Belshaw, Syd Abbot, Ivor

Brown, and Denis Smith - faces I see with names I cannot recall, ah well! At, Turners, I played in the team for 3 seasons, winning championships and trophies. Then as captain of Breach United - what a team with Dick Hogg, the goalie, Les Hodgkinson, Boney Gaynor, and Archie Hallam to name a few! I was chosen to captain Eastwood and District against the German prisoners of war, a team who had never been beaten. Our team got together by Jack Grainger, who gave me my instructions as captain, "YOU HAVE GOT TO WIN!" That was it. We did win! I scored the 1st goal, finding out at a much later date that Bert Trautman, was their goalie.

After this match I was invited to go to Mansfield Town. I never did get into the first team or get any payments. The fact was it was costing me money. I was invited in to another venture. I went back into local football and finished my playing with the Eastwood Community Centre. In one match we played G.R. Turners on New Eastwood Rec. We beat them. I scored the goal that won us the match. My father was still on the committee of that team. He had come as a spectator and picked up my bag. Johnny Chambers, a local character who had suffered an illness as a child, which had left him afflicted, snatched the bag from Dad - he always carried Don's bag!

The first professional match I ever saw was Derby County versus Aston Villa, in 1938. The players were wearing black armbands in memory of Steve Bloomer who had died earlier that week.

The most memorable match for my memory box, without doubt, is the 1966 World Cup Final. Throughout the tournament I declared that England would win the cup. I had the greatest respect and confidence in Alf Ramsey who later became Sir Alfred Ramsey. On the day of the final, 30th July 1966, my wife, son and I arrived in Llandudno; our hotel had no television. We had a snack and then set off around the town. There was slight drizzle in the air but this was no problem; I had plans. It was about 2.00pm. I found what I was looking for - a shop with a television set switched on. The pavement was wide and nearby a typical wayside seat. We carried the seat placing it a couple of feet in front of the window and settled on it. More and more people gathered, the owner of the shop opened the door turned the sound up and asked if we could hear. The weather became fine; it was if we were at a live match. At least a hundred people cheering the same team, joining in the community singing, being brought tea and biscuits; what a start to a holiday! Hours after the kick off, this throng of holidaymakers went round hugging each other, put the seats back to their correct positions, thanked the shopkeeper and finally said their fond farewells. When we set off back to our hotel David said, "Will you buy me a football Dad?" No need to tell you my reply.

Many matches stick in my mind; matches I have played in, matches I have managed and matches where I have been a spectator. The match, which created the most emotion, was when my son was in a schoolboy cup final with 4 grandparents watching. I remember that game well. It was a great game. David played for Devonshire Drive. He scored a goal. The team won the match. Tony Woodcock also played for Devonshire Drive. He later became an International player and also played for Nottingham Forest.

I was at Wembley Stadium for the Nottingham Forest v Luton Town Cup Final and also for Schoolboy Internationals. I got involved with local football curtailing my visiting professional matches until I was invited to visit the Baseball Ground to see the Rams v Chelsea match. Brian Clough was the manager. I was hooked again, supporting Derby at their home matches until Cloughie resigned.

In 1991 I started supporting Eastwood Town home and away. I still get to the home matches but not many away games. I now am a big screen supporter at the local Victory Club spending many happy hours there. What football maniac of my age could ever forget the Cup Final of 1952?! It is mostly called the Mathews final. With three minutes to go Mortenson was fouled on the edge of the penalty box: a barrier of Bolton players lined up as he prepared to take the kick, he spotted a gap, hit the ball hard and true, 3-3. With only 1 minute left Mathews got the ball wide, pulling it inside, a defender swayed outside, another acceleration leaving that defender for dead and cut in; Barrass came to intercept but Mathews slipped the ball to an unmarked Perry who scored the winning goal.

When discussing football I think there will always be a difference of opinion. The actual sentence I found in an article written by Charles Buchan, who was the first one £1000 transfer. 'There will always be a difference of opinion as to whether we of today are playing football as effectively as the line of brilliant exponents of former years such as in the palmy days of Preston North End.' He wrote the article in 1954. He was quoting a book written by Steve Bloomer in 1905 – yes - the same Steve Bloomer for whom the players in that 1938 match were wearing their black armbands.

Now, to a FA Cup tie of March 1974. It concluded after 5 hours playing time and many hours in meetings. On form Second Division Forest were given little chance against First Division Newcastle United at St. James Park. Forest were leading 2-1 at the interval with goals from Ian Bowyer and Liam O'Kane. In the 55th minute Duncan McKenzie was fouled by David Craig. The referee Gordon Kew awarded Forest a penalty, Pat Howard Newcastle centre-half played up and was sent off, George Lyll converted 3-1 to Forest, Newcastle down to 10 men looked doomed. Police stated 300 to 500 spectators invaded the pitch; 2 Forest players were assaulted and the referee ordered all the players to the dressing rooms for safety. 23 people were taken to hospital, 103 others treated at the ground. The police made 39 arrests and took 8 minutes to clear the pitch. The game was resumed; Forest conceded 3 goals in the last 20 minutes. The F.A annulled the result of this match even though Newcastle had been drawn to meet Burnley in the semi-final. The F.A also ordered the match to be replayed on a neutral ground. It took 2 games for Newcastle to proceed to the semi-final, on Monday the 18th March - a 0-0 draw after extra time and 3 days 1-0 to Newcastle - both games at Goodison Park.

I remember another match for a different reason. It was a Cup Final between Nottingham Forest and West Bromwich Albion on the City Ground Nottingham. I cannot remember the date: I am almost certain it was before 1949. The 90 minutes was played, then extra time, then extra extra time; after that the golden goal. Forest scored that goal after 12 minutes. That game had 162 minutes of actual playing time. I watched them all. My Uncle Percy left to get the 6 o'clock train.

A game that was certainly different was played on the old Basin ground behind The Mundy Arms Inn at Marlpool, the year was 1936 it was The Chimney Sweepers of Langley versus The Bakers of Marlpool, I can't remember but other than the ball there was plenty of flour, soot and laughs.

To finish with what about that last game of the season May 1983, at Derby, Rams v Fulham. A win for Derby, they would not be relegated, a win for Fulham they would gain promotion. After 75 minutes, Davidson scored for Derby; some of the crowd invaded the pitch and it was soon cleared. The crowd gathered around the pitch, 5 or 6 deep. A spectator kicked Wilson, a Fulham player, while the ball was in play; the touchlines were no longer visible. The referee, Mr Chadwick from Darwin, blew his whistle for offside: the fans thinking the game was over swarmed the pitch, but 78 seconds of the game remained. The FA ruled the result should stand. Derby County were ordered to improve security. A second Fulham player was injured in the incident, Malcolm Macdonald the

Fulham manager, felt his team should have a replay. Fulham lodged an appeal but got no joy.

I have found that I have played in matches, which I remember nothing of. This is certainly a shock, but I am putting it down to the illness I endured and recovered from in 1993. One of these matches was on the ground used by the Eastwood Town Cricket Club on the Breach, I played for Eastwood Community Centre against Eastwood Miners Welfare beating them. My cousin George Kemp played for them, I don't know if he played that day, I only know I played through reading an old paper.

Birnam Products Football Team

Back Row: Don Brown, Trevor Naylor, David Johnson, Tony Hatton, Unknown, Percy Bower, Geoff Leivers.
Front Row: Mick Buxton, David Brown, Trevor Brough, Unknown, Steve Cope, Pete Kenmuir.

SCHOOLBOY FOOTBALL

I saw him play the game

I saw him play it well

Enthusiasm, endeavour, youth, vigour,

all there

Came the final whistle

all square

Extra time

More to come and go

Still no score

Exhaustion, tired limbs;

penalties to be taken

Exhilaration then

Humiliation

Despair –

He missed!

Is it fair?

I started work on 28th August 1939, 1 week before war was declared on Germany. In 1941, a group of us, myself, Reggie Lee, Jack Carlin, his brother Alf, Freddie Simms, Ron Wood and Stan Grainger decided we would do a bike ride to Abergele in north Wales. We planned to go for the week.

We put Jack in charge because he knew the way and there were no signposts in those days. As we were expecting Germany to invade, there were no names on the Post Offices, streets or Railway stations or any means of finding out where we were. We carried our clothes and food for the week, our tents and all our needs. One lad actually made a trailer. Jack and his brother travelled on a tandem, with Jack at the front.

On the first day we got to a small village just before Chester. We asked the farmer if we could use his field for camping that night. He said everything was ok as long as we didn't have a fire. We didn't have a fire but, we used our Primus heater and something went wrong – flames were all in the wrong places! The heater was hurled into the pond; the oil spread over the top of the pond and then caught fire! For what seemed like ages, the pond was a blazing inferno! We waited in silence, scared stiff. Nothing further happened so after a while we went to our 3-tent camp. In the morning, we all bathed and washed in the adjoining canal. When we emerged from the canal, we collapsed in fits of laughter for we had disturbed the red clay from the bottom and came out looking like red Indians with our skins dyed copper red!

I was appointed cook and kept the job right through the week. The only complaint that I had was that I dished out too much semolina. Food rationing was in force. If you didn't eat what was put in front of you, you were not hungry – it was as simple as that!

The next day, we set off for Abergele and we eventually got there. I reckoned we went many more miles than we needed to have done. We followed the coastline for many a mile – it was truly exciting. We stayed on a campsite for 3 or 4 days and used that for our base camp. We did different trips daily, split into groups and as we wished there was no bickering, squabbles or fights. It was an expedition we could be proud of. We moved camp on the last day but on one of our treks, we set off for Llangollen by way of Horseshoe Pass. What a ride! What excitement! We spent all morning climbing; only an hour or so declining; sheer drops on one side; boulders, rocks, sheep and grass on the other. We had wonderful weather all week and the Pass road was good. We got to the bottom; all except the tandem. We waited and questioned everyone who travelled past us from the same direction we had travelled. No one had seen the tandem or our companions. We waited and waited. At last, when we were beginning to despair, they arrived. They were ok. The trouble had been that with constant use, the hub brake had seized up. They had to cool the brake down and this had taken a fair amount of time. Then they decided to put a bit of lubricant on the brake – they did; BUTTER!

On our last day we cycled from Llangollen to our homes. We made our last stop between Morley and Smalley. We had 1 large tin of jam left and shared it in spoonfuls. What a journey! What an experience! A bike ride of a lifetime and one never to be forgotten!

A short time before this, I had joined the Air Training Corps. I did not want to go into the R.A.F. My first choice had been the Royal Navy as my Dad had been in the Navy and his stories had excited me so I wanted to follow. There were no Sea Cadets locally so I was advised to join the A.T.C. It was great fun. We had square bashing lectures on wireless, radar, navigation, first aid and many other topics. We had plenty of sport, football, cross country running, boxing and gymnastics. I didn't play football for the corps. I was already signed up with Langley Mill Y.C and we were doing quite well. Parties of cadets were stationed on airfields for a week or ten days or so. I was stationed for one of my trips at Digby in Lincolnshire. It was an operational airfield, at the time of Dieppe, to give us Allies, an insight into such attacks. It was a disaster. On our airfield, we had Boulton Paul Defiants, a twin seater, single engine escort fighter. The gunner sat back to back with the pilot in a twin gun turret. We received terrible losses and we saw our broken and crippled aircraft returning with the Canadian lads that flew them. There was much blood and carnage. We were shown the tragedies of war in startling fashion and went to our tents sad and shocked.

Next day, we went on our duties and were quickly into our routines with no time to worry about anything but the tasks we had to undertake. A lesson was there for us to learn a lesson that stands one in good stead for the rest of one's life.

At Digby, Jammy Rowley got a flight in a Defiant. He was in the gun turret with loaded guns. Jammy's first name was Arthur. Things always turned out right for him and he was so lucky, that's why we called him Jammy. The pilot said that Jammy had done ok apart from referring to the floor instead of the ground. He and his brother Ben owned Brinsley Garage. In their spare time, they played cricket and we all played for Eastwood Town together many times. The football club, Langley Mill Y.C was the first team that I played for. We played on the ground off Aldreds Lane at the back of the Bus sheds. We had no changing rooms. We turned up with our strip under our over clothes, peeled the top ones off, put them in a pile in the hedge bottom, ran on to the pitch and got started. Mum and Dad came down to see us once – never again. Hamer Brown got injured; we dragged him to the side and then carried on playing. I didn't know that Mum and Dad were watching – they told me when I got back. I told them that I knew he was alright because I had done my first aid. Anyway, they were not impressed and never came to see me with that team again!

When I was a nipper, Langley Rovers played at that ground. They changed at the Butcher's Arms on Hands Road. The Butcher's Arms is opposite the recreation ground. We called it the 'recca.' We had good games on there, both cricket and football. Everyone was a good bowler because the ball moved all over the place! I always had a bat and ball. I always had a football. I was one of the lucky ones but all the lads got the benefit of my luck.

Don

Chapter Five

Family Life

Mum, Dad and Jean

My Dad, James John Brown's complete working life was spent on the same site, which was G.R. Turner Ltd, an engineering firm, manufacturing railway rolling stock and mining machinery. In its later years it changed hands many times and Dad worked for every firm who took over until British Steel, who owned it, pensioned him off. Dad served in the Royal Navy in the Great War (1914 – 1918) he was in the Royal Navy Volunteer Reserve.

He said it was called the Rather Naughty Very Rude. At the age of 16, Dad became the secretary of the Langley Mill United cricket club. He was awarded two medals when the club won competitions; my brother had one, I had the other. Dad held the position as secretary until he went into the Navy, never to retake it.

He had started courting Mother and that took preference, lucky for all of us who follow. Mother and Dad were married on Christmas Day 1919 at Heanor Church. Mother was Lucy May Parkin the daughter of William and Lucy Parkin. Father was James John Brown the first born to Frederick Ernest and Lucy Brown. On that Christmas Day of 1919, mother's brother Harry gave her away. Grandad Parkin said he didn't want to lose her, so refused to give her away.

Wedding Day 25 Dec 1919

Back Row: Sam Hartshorne, Lizzie Brown, James John Brown, Lucy May Parkin, Eva Brown, Harry Parkin,
Front Row: Unknown bridesmaid, Olive Parkin

Mother was a milliner working in a local shop; in her schooldays she attended the same schools as me in my first formative days. From the beginning of their days together Mum and Dad played tennis and as a youngster I remember going to the tournaments with them, also to courts of Buxton Bros. builders on Hands Road, Langley 50 yards down the road from our old farmhouse.

After their marriage mother and father lived in an old farmhouse 50 yards down the road from Olive Cottage. I lived there until I was 8 years old, when we moved up to Tantum Cottage, staying for 3 years then moving into 114 Lacey Fields Road, a brand new house built by Buxton Bros, which was the last residence of my parents.

I left their home on December 3rd 1949 to make a home for myself, and my bride of that day. The wedding ceremony took place at Saint Mary's Church Eastwood, conducted by the Rev Peter Caporn. The bride was the beautiful Miss Jean Elizabeth Purdy. Her attendants were her cousins, Ida and Alice Roddiss. The best man was my brother Frederick William Brown and the usher, my cousin Stanley Richardson. The reception was held in The Eastwood Community Centre and we spent our honeymoon in Yorkshire. Jean continued to work in the factory of Wolsey at Kimberley until the spring of 1954, prior to the birth of our son, David, then returned into employment in 1966.

We left the old farmhouse in 1932 moving into Tantum Cottage 100 yards higher up Hands Road on the same side, Grandad Parkin's Olive Cottage lay midway between. I had enjoyed my first years immensely but Tantum Cottage soon dispelled any fears I had of moving. Tantum Cottage - I never did see the deeds of this abode, it must have been built at the times of the Howitts of Heanor and being just about 200 or 300 yards from their dwelling, given this name. It was a four bedroom double fronted house, with upstairs toilet and bathroom. It overlooked the Erewash Valley into Nottinghamshire at the rear and a across the road, the smallholding at the front. Dad built a greenhouse at the bottom of the garden. At the rear of the residence was a raised patio, which could exit from both sides. On the left hand side path was a series of brick buildings stretching halfway down to Dad's greenhouse. It was great. People stayed with us, it was a boarding house. I suppose now we would call it a guesthouse. We left there in 1936, moving to 114 Lacey Fields Road.

NEW SEASON

The smell of the newly mown grass,

The sound of the leather on willow,

The clang of the bell,

The walk of the umpires,

The team who are going to field

troop out followed by the two who are going to bat.

The opening bowler marks out his run

No.1 takes his guard.

The opening bowler loosens up

No.1 gazes round at the field.

The bowler starts his run,

over goes his arm

IT'S BEGUN

THE NEW SEASON.

Shipley Boat Cricket Club

George Webster, Fred Bagguley, Ron Jeffries, Don Brown, Gerry Smith, Les Fretwell, Eric Evans, Ron Durose, Alan Hunt, Gordon Davies, Walter Campion. Ron Sandby on the steps

Eastwood Town Cricket Club

Back Row: Umpire, Brian Parson, Ben Rowley, Arthur Rowley, Arthur Booth, Ken Astle, Umpire
Front Row: Alf Ross, Jeff Astle, Jim Astle, Ron Durose, Reg Brown, Don Brown

DOCTOR'S APPOINTMENT

It was a beautiful sunny morning as I headed off for my 9.10am appointment with Dr Ashworth. I had missed the bus and so caught a taxi to the surgery. How times have changed since I moved into Eastwood in 1949! In those days, Dr Gladstone's surgery was in a shed beside his house at the top of Church Street. Walt Pollard was his secretary. Walt knew every patient and would have their card ready as soon as they arrived.

Dr Gladstone was a surgeon. He operated on me twice in his surgery. My son, David, recalls how, when he was injured whilst playing rugby, and went to the surgery, Dr Gladstone raised him up by his head, pulling his neck back into place. David had no more problems.

My first operation there was for the removal of a growth at the side of my neck. During the procedure, I felt that I was going to pass out and I said to Dr Gladstone, "I'm going!" "You're going nowhere," he replied as he flung the window open. He was right; I went nowhere. He proceeded to cut out the problem growth and, dropped it into a bucket. He then applied six stitches to the wound, went into the waiting room and told one of his patients, whom he knew had a car, to take me home, but not before he asked me, "Do you want a fag?" I said, "No thanks."

The second operation was to remove a splinter, actually a blade of glass from between my thumb and index finger of my left hand. He kept pulling and the straw-like splinter kept coming. It must have been two inches long! "Bloody hell!" he exclaimed, "I've never seen one like this before!"

Dr Gladstone was the president of our cricket club – a great character, not a very good cricketer but a damn good sport! Golf was his game. We had a president's game. One day Dr Gladstone and I were talking. He said it was more difficult to hit a golf ball with a club than a ball with a bat. "Don't be ridiculous!" I said. He promptly took me outside the Old Shipley Boat pub and took the golf clubs out of his car boot. He placed a ball on the tee, a club in my hand and said, "Go on then!" I'd never held a golf club before! I got the feel of the club by swishing it about a bit, then set myself swinging. I hit the ball. It didn't soar in the air but I sent it a fair distance. "You didn't hit it straight!" he shouted. "That's not the point," I replied. It didn't go directly in front of me, but it was hit! We went back into the pub.

When we played cricket, I was the wicket keeper and my cousin George was going to bowl to Dr

Gladstone. "Give him a good'un," I told George. George, a medium pace bowler ran in, gave a good length delivery, pitching just wide of off peg, where the ball turned and took the middle peg. Dr Gladstone turned, looked at me, we laughed together and said nothing. George said, "Sorry Doc, but we can't have our president out at first ball, can we? Carry on!" He continued his innings and also as our president.

BRIDGES

My favourite bridge is The Forth Rail Bridge and in my estimation, one of the world's greatest engineering achievements.

More than a mile and a half long, it towers 450 feet above its foundations. Giant columns stride across the turbulent estuary of the river Forth, spanning the distance between Fife and the Lothians. The secret of the Bridges stability is in the strength of its foundations. Tragically 57 lives were lost in the seven years it took to construct. When it was opened in 1890 it changed the face of the East Coast railway system. It has carried main line trains every day since. A team of maintenance engineers are on duty 24 hours a day, every day. It is the same with the team of painters, keeping it to me as a thing of beauty as well as its main purpose.

One of the local bridges known to us locals as *forty bridges* was demolished a while ago now; I think in the 1970's. It was on the Great Northern Railway Line that runs from Nottingham Victoria terminating at Pinxton. The line was closed by Dr Beeching. I travelled on the last train from Nottingham on that line getting off at the Newthorpe and Greasley station, which was in New Eastwood.

New Eastwood is the village I moved into in 1949, the main street one side in Greasley the other in the Urban Council District of Eastwood. After the closure of the railway much of its path was turned into the Eastwood By pass known as the A610 road. The Forty Bridges was a viaduct. I never did count the arches, but guess there must have been approximately forty. Here are photos of me jumping off the bridge - no wonder I have bad knees!

Don Brown jumping off Forty Bridges

While walking on the towpath of the Nottingham Canal, I took a photo of a train using the bridge. How I wish I had written the date on the back of the said photo!

Trent Bridge is another lovely bridge I have sailed under many times and have crossed many, many more. The suspension bridge a little further up the river is also good to view.

CANALS

Jessop surveyed 15 miles from the River Trent in Nottingham to Langley Mill. Work was started in 1792 and completed in 1796.

The Nottingham Canal and the Erewash Canal ran more or less parallel for about 7 miles. Railway competition soon affected the Nottingham Canal and in 1855 it was sold to the Railway Company, who had bought the Grantham Canal in 1854. The Canal closed in 1937. A short stretch is still navigable and it's path easily traced. It joined with the Cromford and Erewash Canal at Langley Mill.

Up to the 1950's the Nottingham Canal was referred to as the Top Cut and the Erewash Canal as the Bottom Cut. At New Eastwood the Top Cut, the Bottom Cut and the Great Northern Railway ran parallel.

A path by the Moon and Stars pub ran over the railway line. Between the lines, 2" thick planks were laid so that wheelbarrows, prams and bikes could be pushed over the lines without difficulty. The track of the Great Northern is now the A610

Eastwood Bye Pass. New Eastwood was served by it's own station, called Newthorpe and Greasley on the Pinxton line.

The journey to Nottingham Victoria took about 15 minutes. After crossing the line, the footpath went through a kissing stile and then down to the Top Cut, which was crossed by using a swing bridge. To get down to the Bottom Cut, the path went through a field known as Roker Park. At the top of the field was a grey round building, which was a powder keg owned by Skeltons the Chemists. The stored powder was used by the quarries and the pits.

A path led to the bottom left of the field with Gudgeon Hole to the bottom right. Over the ditch, through the stile was the Bottom Cut; right for Langley Mill; left for Shipley Boat. At Shipley Boat, past Noon's Knacker yard and then over the cut, by way of the bridge or the lock on the other side was the wharf of Woodside Incline, where coal from the Woodside Colliery was loaded on to the barges. The headstocks of Woodside Colliery still stand and are in the American Adventure theme park. This theme park was closed down in 2008.

Chapter Six

Working Life

I joined G.R. Turners, a well-established engineering company and started working in my father's office. He was the timekeeper. I soon made my first mistake. He handed me some papers saying put these on the file. I thought he said fire! Soon after that I became an engineering apprentice, working with highly skilled tradesmen many of these skills had been handed down from father to son. One of these fathers was Bill Etherton, the foreman of the Smith shop where his son plied his trade.

I was taught the trades of a blacksmith, machinist, fitter, diesinker, plater, draughtsman, moulder, core maker. After 7 years of this, I finished my apprenticeship and worked in the maintenance department of the factory. The factory consisted of Smith shop, Saw mill, Foundry, Pattern shop, Machine shop, Die shop, Wagon shop, Fitting shop, Frame shop, Welding and gas cutting area, painting and packing areas, also large railway sidings and steel stock storage areas. It had three crane bays, which housed four cranes, the longest bay was about 200 yards long and 30 yards wide, and two cranes traversed its track. Near the bottom end of the track a pit was sunk, it was twenty yards square and seven yards deep, bricked on the sides and guarded by rails with a gated entrance and a steel ladder. It was called the bear pit and used when tall objects were manufactured. When I started my employment at Turners it was mostly raw materials brought in and as time went by I noticed a decline in this and an increase in manufactured items. The decline continued, I left Turners in 1960 becoming a maintenance engineer at McCarthy (Macs) a brick making company and I became the plant manager.

It was with Macs I faced and completed my largest and most difficult task as an engineer. A Rushton digger needed it's king pin replacing, which entailed the lifting arm being removed, the cab being hoisted off, the caterpillar track removed then the complete bottom body inverted, raised and supported for the removal of the pin. My staff for this was a digger driver, my crane, which was a digger, two labourers and myself. On the day of the fitting of the new pin came, I had three bosses, all McCarthy's; Mr John the top man, Mr Pat, John's son, and John's brother Mr Michael. They did not turn up, and yes I was the fall guy. I had a large tank for containing liquid nitrogen in which I was going to immerse the pin, causing the pin to diminish in size thus enabling me to fit it into its housing. I spent much time trying to achieve this, but had no joy. I sent the gas container lorry back to its depot, phoned Ruston, telling them I could not get it down to size. They informed me that they thought I was going to machine it size but we did not have a machine large enough for the job. I measured the housing and sent the measurements along with the pin. The pin came back; the job was finished. The steam, the tension, the excitement the fulfilment, I shall never forget. I had 4 years with McCarthy's averaging between 80 to 100 hours a week. I left to join Bonser, an engineering firm, to become a project producer, making two fork trucks, then tooling up, as production increased, I designed and produced a production line along with the storage pallets. When things were going well I was promoted to Plant Manager I stayed with Bonsers for four years, getting out of industry into education. Their chief designer was Harry Carnell, and he was drafting a fork truck, using a David Brown tractor as its base. A tractor uses 2 small wheels at the front and two large wheels behind, a fork truck is opposite. Harry was drawing, I making. He designed a 48-cubit weight casting for the rear, counter balance for the load. At this time my only lifting device was a pulley block, designed to lift no more than one ton. I had lifted the casting about a foot, packing up about every 6 inches or so. The chain broke. I lifted the casting to the height required with jacks, pushing the wheeled chassis into position manually.

Eventually I completed the first 2 Bonser fork trucks. They were exported to Karachi, so into production we went. The first 100 hundred trucks had to have their gear change levers bent by hand. The gear change lever was the last jig to be made.

Before this, I had designed and produced an assembly line, with the component racks beside it, adjustable welding tables and much more. I became the Plant Manager. Bonsers was a non-union firm. I found myself being called to work all hours, climbing on to the roof, the crane and all manner of breakdowns so I decided to leave. When I went to John Bonser to hand him my resignation he asked, "How much do you want, Don?" I replied, "This is not about money, John." He smiled. Many times after I contacted him for references and he obliged. Sadly John died a young man.

Chapter Seven

Landmarks in Life

The Eastwood Church Fire

I was retained as a fireman at Eastwood Fire Station. Tuesday nights was our practice night and we usually stayed until around 9.00pm.

On Tuesday 5th March 1963, everyone had left the station apart from Tom Parsons and me. At that time the station was in the Eastwood Urban District Council yard, Church Street about 100 – 150 yards from the church.

The alarm was raised. Tom started up the fire engine. I took the message and threw the other firemens' uniform, helmets, boots, coats, belts and axes into the engine. We trailed a pump and carried 600 gallons of water. I knew the other firemen had gone to the pub.

We arrived at the church. Tom managed the pump. I went into the church with the hose, fed from the 600 gallons on board. The other lads were there in minutes. Bill Wardle, a leading fireman took charge. He asked for pumps to be increased to 7. I took a hose from the now plentiful water supply. We fought the fire from within but we were not winning. The Fire Chief from Nottingham arrived. I was with Mick Henry and the stone was now breaking away from the building. A large piece of slate fell and stuck into Mick's helmet and we were ordered out. I took my position on the fuel tank on the Church Walk side of the building and was there until about 3.00am when damping down arrived. We then went up the tower and surveyed the damage. Damping down continued all the next day.

One day when I drove the engine to Nottingham, they all said that they had "never gotten to Nottingham so quick." I have so many memorable times of the fire service, exciting funny and dangerous but nonetheless very rewarding.

Eastwood man rescued his three neighbours

AWARD FOR COURAGE IN FIRE

AN Eastwood man who rescued three-neighbours from a smoke-filled house was awarded the Society for the Protection of Life from Fires framed certificate at today's meeting of Nottinghamshire County Council.

presenting the award to Mr. Donald Brown, of 118 Chewton Street, Eastwood, the chairman, Ald. Mrs. Anne Yates, congratulated him on his courage.

She said that the rescue was in the early hours of April 26, when Mr. Royce Marriott fell asleep on a settee downstairs with a lighted cigarette in his hand at his home at 114 Chewton Street. The fire spread and his parents were prevented from entering the room due to thick smoke so they returned downstairs and raised the alarm.

Ex-fireman

Mr. Brown heard cries for help and rescued Mr. and Mrs. Marriott from the first floor. Then went twice to the ground floor with buckets of water to try and extinguish the fire.

He then learned that Royce Marriott was still in the room and went in a third time to help him, with the assistance of a neighbour.

Mr. Brown was helped by neighbours but it was due to his

Mr. Brown at today's presentation

personal efforts and organising ability that the rescues were effective.

Ald. Mrs. Yates told Mr. Brown who is an ex-retained fireman, "No dout your training as a fireman stood you in good stead, but that would have been quite useless without your own courage."

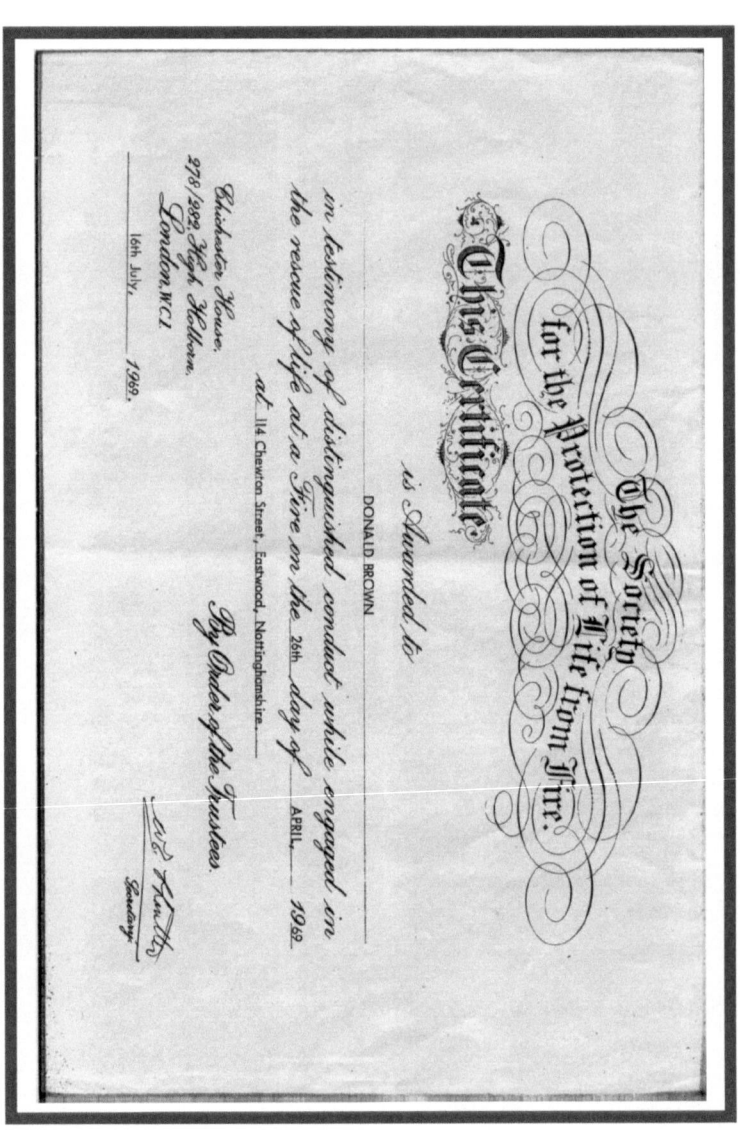

I joined South East Derbyshire College in 1968 as a technician; I was a lecturer for evening classes. I was employed by Derbyshire County Council at the Heanor branch, part of which was the old Grammar School. I worked there for 10 years leaving to become a technician with Notts County Council stationed at Eastwood Comprehensive School. My first job was to change all the machines from English standards to Metric. I enjoyed my employment and I was involved with the students much more than at Heanor. Their ages ranged from 11 to 18 years and being the only engineer in that establishment I was able to sort all the problems out.

DEATH OF A LOVED ONE

Brush away the tears

Hide the fears

All can be well

That's what the Gospels tell.

Wipe away the tears

Shed the fears

All will be well

Let your heart swell.

Put on a smile

It's worthwhile

Face up to life

You've lost the treasure

You! Only you know!

My Jean

BROWN EYES

Sitting

Park bench after closing time

Making poems

Saying poems to listening trees

Still sitting

Seeing you

Brown eyes

Laughing

YOU!

SOLITUDE

I'm in despair and yet I care.

I love my Jeannie and always will.

She was mine, I want her still

I cannot have

I never will

I love her more each day. What a price I pay!

She's in my heart but not in my arms

I want to join her

My heart is full

Life with her was never dull

I cannot leave you, I do not want to

Yet, I cannot hold you

Jeannie, sweetheart, I love you still

I know I always will.

I'm coming to you, when I can.

I started at Eastwood in 1978 and retired in August 1990. Jean and I took our two granddaughters on holiday to Skegness and we had a wonderful time, but within a year Jean was dead. That was the 31st July 1991.

I was friendly with Steve Walker, a young curate. He said, "Let's pray, Don," so we did. It was Steve who did the praying I just said Amen. The next day I met Brian Owen, Headmaster of the Eastwood Comprehensive School. He asked me how I was and I answered by saying that I had no purpose in life. "How would you like to come back to school?" he asked. I told him that I would love to. He then added, "I have no money." I went to see my former Head of Department who said that I could go back all day every day. I didn't want to take on too much so decided to do two days per week. In two weeks I was doing full time but I was out every night.

I returned as an unpaid classroom assistant. I started in the Woodwork Room at Walker Street, Eastwood Notts. It was intake for the juniors of the local area and among them was my eldest granddaughter. I was there until that period of which I wrote in a Night to Remember.

Working at Eastwood Comprehensive

This was the deepest depression I had ever been in. I sat in the park on my way home from the football club. It was well after midnight. I walked back home from there and on reaching home, after more tears, I wrote and prayed, then went to sleep.

The Park

The park has a voice

If you listen

Above the turmoil of your mind

If you listen

It's late, after midnight

On a summer's night; pub closed hours ago.

I'm in despair, yet I care

I talk to anything that listens.

I love her, always will

Mine. Want her still

Cannot have, never will.

In my heart, not my arms

Kissed on the cheek with love

Like dew kissing the flowers

I stoop to smell, hold and listen.

Listen, listen, listen.

On Tuesday 8th June 1993, I took a trip to Skegness with the Women's union.

- a beautiful day; sun shining all the while. I thought it was going to be hard for me returning to Skegness. Jeannie, Rebecca, Julie and myself had a wonderful time there on our last holiday when we were all together.

Looking at the pictures, Jeannie was a picture of health and she was so beautiful yet when we started on our holiday together, she was so sad. David had to console her before he left us. We shall never know her innermost thoughts. Things she said live in my heart. "Don't talk about clouds, Don." Why? "They remind me of death." What did she know? I recapture her sayings yet I can't hear her voice. What a lucky man I was! Out of the millions of people on this earth, I was the one she chose to shower her love on. She worshipped the ground I walked on and I could do nothing wrong. I used to irritate her with my eccentric actions and forgetfulness. She was patient and kind beyond belief and her support to me could never be strengthened. When I was a crippled with arthritis, she cried each night for me. When I found the diet that took the pain away she put up the money and made sure everything I needed was at hand.

I relied on her so much. I tried to repay her and I think of the joy in her lovely brown eyes when I gave her a pleasant surprise. She did not want to leave me and I could not go with her. How lucky I was to have her. I live a different life now and had a good day in Skegness.

A new day dawned and what a beautiful day I had. It started and finished with thanks. From then on everything I did was a joy. Thanks for going to school – what strength it had given me.

Blackpool Barbershop

In the early days of losing Jean, I took David, Yvonne, Rebecca and Julie along with my friend, Walter to Blackpool.

Jean and I had only been to Blackpool on a day trip and it had rained all day. This time I was certain that nothing would cause me to think of anything that would upset me, with memories aroused, for there were none to remember. I went to Blackpool in each school holiday, apart from Christmas holidays and took Walter with me at least once a year.

On one occasion, when Walter and I had gone to Blackpool together, he wanted his hair cutting. We set off to find a barber. After a while of searching, we found one.

The barber was a young lady and as soon as we walked into the shop, she greeted us with, "I've been waiting for you all morning." When I replied, "You don't know us!" she explained that she needed to go to the toilet and wanted someone to turn up so that she could leave the shop. She then left the shop, with cash till and everything! "Get in the chair," I told Walter. He did and I cut his hair.

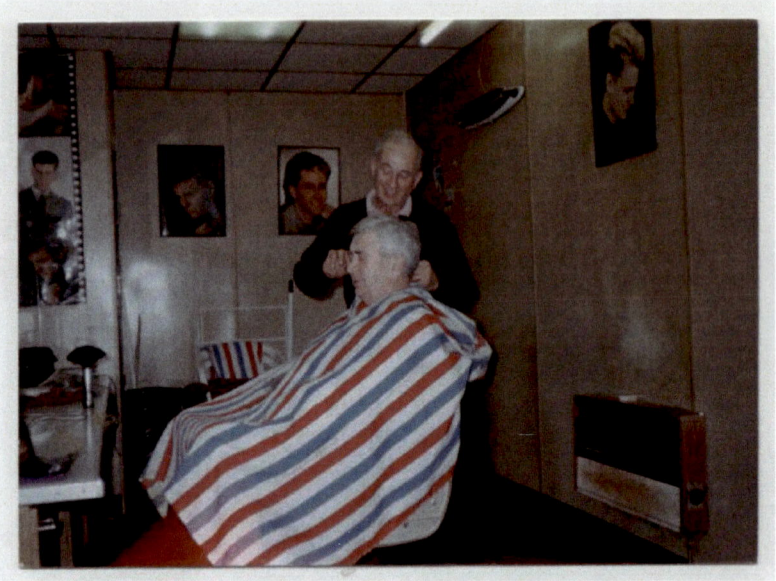

The young lady came back and saw what I had done. She took this photo and invited me to join her as her assistant!

Chapter Eight

The Awakening

When Jean died I did not think I wanted to live, I could see no reason and had no desire. I went out every night hitting the bottle. I went to church on Sundays. I helped with a youth club; I got no satisfaction from that.

The night that changed it all

After 2 years of this, I was awakened by a pain in my head. It was dark and the middle of the night. I had no idea of the time; I unlocked my front door, put the phone on the front room carpet then phoned the doctors. It was an answering machine, giving me another number. I rang that number and on hearing a proper voice I gave my name and my address, adding that my front door is unlocked. She asked, "Do you want an ambulance?" I replied, "I don't know what I want." I then put myself in the recovery position and passed out. I awoke briefly to find two men putting me on a stretcher. My front door was open; the sun was shining, the next door but one neighbour was standing by my gate and that was the last I remembered for some days.

Three weeks later I was discharged from Hospital knowing that I did want to live. I am living and enjoying life.

PARTY TIME

I've thrown a party for the birds

Only a handful

What a party!

Gatecrashers

All!

Just dropped in

from different places,

different colours,

different faces,

wined

dined

danced

even bathed together;

dried in the sun.

Why just them?

Tomorrow

I'll have another party.

July 1993

I'm home, reflecting on past times. It's just 4 weeks since I left hospital. Life stood still, yet I have seen so much. I remember leaving home, yet not much after that for about a fortnight.

It was a mixture of dream and fantasy; then I awoke to reality.

I could see. I could talk and know what I was saying. I could understand. I could walk.

From now on every day is a bonus. I will try to do nothing but good and bring pleasure to all who meet me. I am thankful and it is good to know that so many people care for me. The cards sent to me gave me so much inspiration and hope.

Life is good.

Being ill made me a better man, made me realize I wanted to live. How hard the hospital staff had worked to give me life! I will be forever grateful. On arriving home and unpacking I found a scrap of paper which I had written, 'this is my first time in hospital as a patient, I must confess I am enjoying being looked after, spoilt; my every whim answered but I realize it must change. I shall drive myself, get well and back into circulation!

Poetry and painting along with sketching are my favourite pastimes and hobbies. The dictionary defines poetry as the art or work of the poet; one of the fine arts, which expresses the imagination and feelings in sensuous, rhythmic language. This leads me to share with you, my poem Painting and Poetry.

PAINTING AND POETRY

Words floating like petals,

fanned by a breeze of musical notes,

bringing delight, inspiration, creation.

Eyes close, pictures form;

then from heart, brain, mind, arm to hand,

pen to paper, brush to canvas;

a poem or painting for more to know.

PAINTING is SILENT POETRY.

POETRY is PAINTING that SPEAKS.

Chapter Nine

A New Lease of Life

Pig at Leisure

A word from Don

When we speak or write, we represent ideas and feelings with words.

When we paint, we represent ideas and feelings with colours, shape, lines and tones.

Just as we have different languages to speak and write, so we have different styles (languages) when we paint.

There are many languages/styles in painting. Just as when learning and understanding a language, when we look at a painting, we have to learn and understand the style. Then we can appreciate all the things that the artist is trying to portray to us as well as appreciating all the qualities of the painting. Painting is like poetry. It has form. Form can be used to convey things we recognise along with ideas and feelings – Just like poetry.

Make the best of what you've got

while you have

No matter what you lose, you've had;

Love and cherish.

When you lose, you still will have

Not the same,

but in your heart

What you love

will never part.

I write to an old lady in Lincoln. She does not enjoy writing so she phones me. One day she rung me up and told me that I had spelt her name wrong. "There are two ll's in Phyllis and you've only put one!" "I've knocked the L out of you and you never felt a thing," I replied. We laughed together. This is the poem inspired by that conversation.

What a difference a letter makes

If gold be your aim

take L out it,

Look what you've got.

Gold is better than gilt

L out of gilt,

Left with a worthless person.

L out of lone – still one.

L out of plain, pain

L out of rule, rue the day.

But L out of lover – it's over!

SALLY

I saw her beauty as she sat there

Lovely smiling face, long golden hair

Sally, playing the piano.

I watched and listened,

her fingers floating over keys;

music giving feelings of delight.

Sally read – wonderful reader

Enthralled with music, words and beauty

I stroll to the table.

Sally joins me. "Shall we play chess?"

"Later Mate," she shouts excitedly

I look into her eyes

We laugh together.

SALLY'S BLIND.

THE TELEPHONE

What makes me answer the phone whenever it rings?
No matter what I'm doing, I answer the bloody thing.
Test Match Special, very first ball, just started a meal –
Uninvited stranger butts in, gives me his spiel!
Am I expecting Prince Charming or even a lottery win?
I don't really know, the phone may go in the bin!
But wait!
That contraption brought action when I lay helpless
ALONE
Thanks for the telephone.

MESSAGES

Do you know
the message we pass
each time we pay
with coins from our hand:
The coins of England, Scotland and Wales?

The coin of England
written in Latin
"An ornament and a safeguard"
and then on the Welsh coin
written in Welsh,
"True I am to my country,"
and so to Scotland,
again in Latin,
"No one provokes me with impunity."

Now to the two pound piece,
Sir Isaac Newton's famous line,
"standing on the shoulders of giants."

Did you know?
If you didn't
Now you do.

Decus et Tutamen – English
Pliedial wyf im gi – Welsh
Nemo me impune lacessit – Scottish

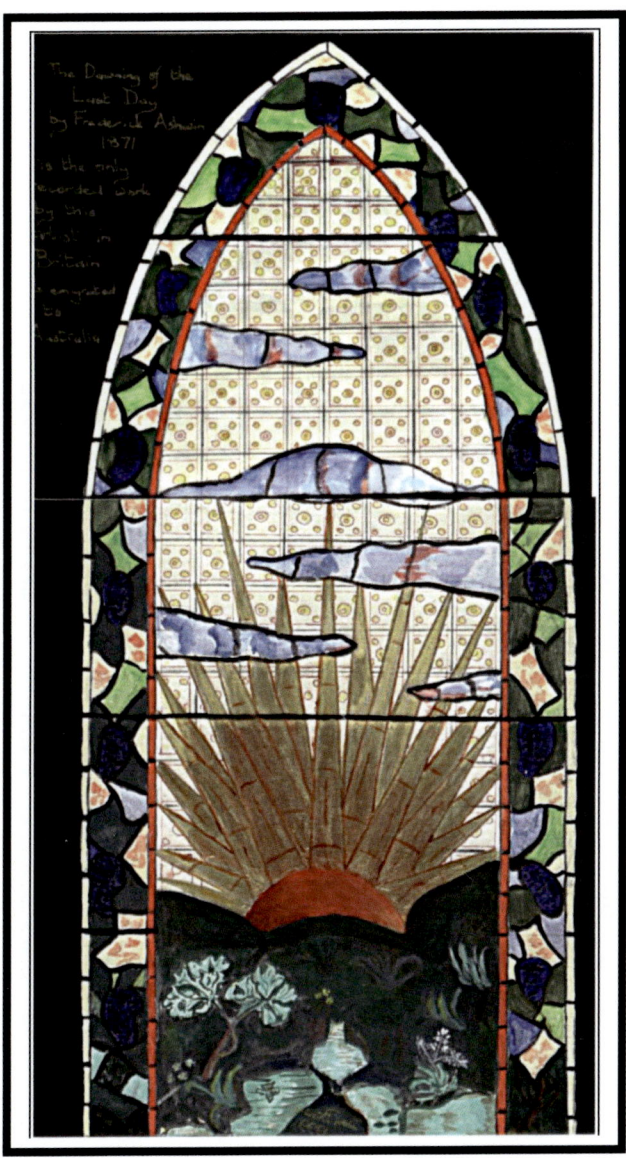

Holy Trinity

God in three persons - Holy Trinity

All three to know

Our Father in heaven

The son in the manger

The spirit in our hearts;

Walk with these in mind

Spread the message with the actions.

These thoughts inspire

You'll never walk alone

Never be lonely, never be sad

though tears still roll down the cheeks

when alone.

Thank you God, the Father, The Son and God

the Holy Ghost.

Good Friday

A day of solitude and sadness - I am alone except for the nearness of Jesus. He has given me the greatest comfort and shown me the way.

Today is the day that Jesus died; it is sad for that yet it is a day for rejoicing, for this is the day that made resurrection possible and so gave us the essence of our Christian faith. They were not villains or rogues who killed Jesus, but ordinary people.

When we look on Jesus, we always go back to the times of 2000 years ago. Should we not try to look at him in modern times? Would we have believed his doctrines? Would we have looked on his miracles as trickery? I do not know but every problem I come up against, I think of Jesus and wonder what would he have done? Do I think too deeply?

I know this. If it had not been for my faith, I would be in a more turbulent state than I am.

Easter

Good Fridays have been around for 2000 years, but Easter Mondays were born in 1872. Easter Day is the Sunday following the first full moon after 21st March.

I attended an Easter service at St Mary's Church, Eastwood. It was a satisfying experience; sad but mindful with reverence. It was a joint service with the Baptists and the parishioners from both churches read the lessons. The Curate led the service. As I sat and listened to the lessons, my eyes were fixed on the wooden cross, which is a fixture in the Parish Church. I thought of the vital importance of Christianity and the Easter story to civilisation; a contribution we ignore and neglect at our peril. I remained transfixed on the cross as I heard the story, which I have heard for over 70 years.

There are times that I have wept listening and seeing the story. I love the story and yet I ask myself why do we have the things that make us question? I believe that the strongest protection we have against the evils and perils of the world are Christian ethics and the Christian belief in the supreme importance of the individual soul. The old religion had much to commend them but they would never admit that the prophet, the thief, the people with their children in the pub garden or the blokes in the pub with their pint pots watching football on the big screen or the women playing bingo are of equal and infinite significance.

Christianity has been at the base of our literature for many years, debating in much of its writings. You can't ignore it. It had its effect on many of our political beliefs causing Tory politicians like Wilberforce to fight for the abolition of slavery. I do not know John Newton's political persuasion but he was a slave trader and his preaching converted him. He is best known for writing the hymn, Amazing Grace. He found the love of God and wanted to share it and give it. He wanted to be a minister and eventually became Curate of St Mary of the Nativity, Lombard Street, London. He later became vicar and rector. The ideals of the Labour Party come in their best form, not from Marx and Engels, but from the lapels of the dissenters.

Politicians do not like to be reminded of Christian ethics and when they are, they often react by criticising the clergy, vicars, bishops etc or by saying the church is far too otherworldly to bother with politics. I would think that 'blessed are the poor' is the quote they wished Jesus had never said! The number of the congregation was pitiful. What a difference from Easter Day or

Christmastime. John Betjeman's 'Diary of a church mouse' springs to mind!

How sad it would be if the Churches stay empty – converted to other things! Where else could I sit surrounded by serenity and history, thinking about the unsolvable mysteries of life and forget the problems of the day.

Faith

Christians, we need to go out and meet people. We must break out of the holy huddle where the only people we know are Christians. We should spend as much time as possible with people in all walks of life and spread the word by example, words and actions; not by preaching; not by putting on shows but by living amongst.

When at work or play how should a Christian pursue success in a world of cutthroat competition? To compete, to defeat opponents and to outwit rivals are considered essential survival skills for most who seek success in this dog eat dog world.

Jesus did not teach his followers to be ruthless or relentless, but rather he emphasised the importance of sharing, helping, serving and loving your neighbour.

So is success out of the reach of Christians? No! Christ made it clear that followers, as individuals, were to be productive and useful members of society.

A follower of Christ should be a positive influence, setting an example as Christ himself did. The right kind of success brings appreciation and approval from God. There can be nothing more important than that. We can and must let Christ work in us.

Strive to make the most of the gifts he has given us. This is not a guarantee of an abundance of fame and fortune. It will give us a satisfying success; the kind that pleases God. Make that success your goal and all will be well.

DESIDERATA

Go placidly amid the noise and the haste, and remember what peace there may be in silence.

As far as possible, without surrender be on good terms with all persons. Speak your truth quietly and clearly, and listen to others, even the dull and ignorant, they too have their story.

Avoid loud and aggressive persons; they are vexatious to the spirit. If you compare yourself to others you may become vain or bitter for always there will be greater or lesser persons than yourself.

Enjoy your achievements as well as your plans. Keep interested in your own career however humble, it is a real possession in the changing fortunes of time.

Exercise caution in your business affairs, for the world is full of trickery. But let this not blind you to what virtue there is, many people strive for high ideals, and everywhere life is full of heroism.

Be yourself. Especially do not feign affection. Neither be cynical about love, for in the face of all aridity and disenchantment it is as perennial as the grass.

Take kindly the counsel of the years, gracefully surrendering the things of youth.

Nurture strength of spirit to shield you in sudden misfortune. But do not distress yourself with dark imaginings. Many fears are born of fatigue and loneliness.

Beyond a wholesome discipline be gentle with yourself, you are a child of the universe, no less than the trees and the stars, you have a right to be here. If it is not clear to you, no doubt the universe is unfolding as it should.

Therefore be at peace with God whatever you conceive Him to be, and whatever your labours and aspirations in the noisy confusion of life, keep peace with your soul. With all its sham, drudgery and broken dreams, it is still a beautiful world. Be cheerful strive to be happy.

Many people believe DESIDERATA was found in Old Saint Paul's Church, Baltimore, America, many years ago but it was not. It was written by Max Ehrmann. He was born in Terre Haute, Indiana on 26th September 1872, the fifth and last child of Maximilian Ehrmann senior and Barbara Lutz Ehrmann who had emigrated from Bavaria in the late 1840's. Max Ehrmann also wrote more than twenty books. Some critics say his work is too sentimental. To me it has a fascinating powerful simplicity.

A legal case in the 1970's concerning the legal ownership of the 1927 copyright of DESIDERATA resulted in it being declared belonging to public domain. Ehrmann died in 1945 being described, as passionate about spiritual wholeness, peace, simplicity, and social justice. He was heard to say, "I know not when, but I contracted a disease I cannot shake off." The disease was IDEALISM.

SLAVERY

In 2007 the Royal Mint issued the two-pound piece, celebrating the abolishment of slavery 200 years earlier. The Mint's brief was very specific to commemorate not the abolishment of slavery itself but a more limited yet crucial step in that direction, namely the 1807 Act, which effectively abolished the slave trade within Britain and its colonies.

The British anti-slavery campaign to end the transatlantic slave trade awakened a passion in people to obtain justice for their fellow human beings. Although Britain did not initiate the transatlantic slave trade, throughout the eighteenth century it came to perfect and dominate it. Britain, however, was instrumental in abolishing this most ubiquitous institution.

Sugar production was the impetus for slavery, with the African people being taken from their native lands and forced aboard dangerously overcrowded ships with inadequate food and water. If they were fortunate enough to survive the journey to the Caribbean or the Americas, they then ended up on sugar plantations, often working in the scorching heat with insufficient food supplies. Some ten to twenty per cent of the slaves died during each sea transportation and many more within a few years of beginning this life of hard labour.

Those who supported the slave trade portrayed Africans as subhuman savages, but this could not have been further from the truth. Sophisticated cultures had flourished in Africa before the arrival of Europeans. One namely, Olaudah Equiano, a former slave, earned enough money to buy his freedom. He wrote his autobiography and campaigned arduously against slavery and together with activists like Thomas Clarkson, Granville Sharp and William Wilberforce, brought about the end to the whole inhumane business.

The two-pound coin was designed by David Gentleman, who was born in 1930. He grew up in Hertford and studied at the Royal College of Art. His work has included wood engravings for press advertisements, drawings for newspapers, posters for London Transport, paperback covers for Penguin books, 100 stamp designs for the Royal Mail, a platform-length mural at Charing Cross Underground station and many more illustrations for books. His designs of coins, for the Mint, graphically portray his thoughts.

JOHN NEWTON

John Newton was born in 1725.

His father was a sea Captain and his mother a devout Christian. John's mother died just before his 7th birthday. His father was at sea until a year later. His father remarried and John went to boarding school. When he was 11 years old, he went to sea as a cabin boy.

In 1742, work was arranged for him in Jamaica, but he had fallen in love and so went into hiding to avoid the trip to Jamaica. His plan backfired and he was press-ganged onto a Man of War ship. Knowing the Admiral, John's father tried to get his son released. He failed but he did manage to get him promoted. In no time, John was in trouble when he deserted his ship. While on foot, enjoying his freedom, he was spotted by a group of soldiers who suspected he had jumped ship. They took him back to the ship, which he had deserted, where he was then put into irons, publicly whipped and demoted. When the boat set sail, John was on duty as an ordinary seaman.

In despair, with only the thoughts of his sweetheart and a great desire to murder the Captain preventing him from throwing himself overboard, John changed ship at Madeira. He sailed on to Sierra Leone, where the Captain of this new ship, died. John feared that he might be transferred to another Man of War ship and so acquired his discharge and took a position with an English slave trader. While his employer was away on business, John fell ill and was subject to great impatience and ridicule from this master's mistress. In his narrative, he wrote, 'my distress has been so great as to compel me to go by night and pull up roots in the plantation. If caught, I would be punished as a thief. I have even eaten roots to destroy the evidence.' When his master returned John complained about his treatment but got no sympathy. When he was fit to resume his duties on the slave ship, he went on board and was promptly locked on deck day and night in all kinds of weather. A bowl of rice was his only ration of food for the day.

When he was 22 years old, John got transferred to another trader, where he received much better treatment and was even given responsibility. The trader, along with John, patrolled the beaches looking for ships to ply their trade. One day on spotting a ship and signalling that trade was being sought, by lighting a fire, they got an immediate response. The Captain came ashore in a canoe. One of his first questions was if they knew of a John Newton!

On hearing of his son's plight, John's father had asked his friends to help him. John reflected much later in his life that had that ship passed one quarter of an hour sooner, he would have died as the wretch he had lived.

On the homeward journey, with not much to do, he picked up a book entitled 'The imitation of Christ' by Thomas A Kempis. He thought deeply. He knew that he was on a course of most horrid impiety. Not content with common oaths and vows, he invented new ones every day. On going to bed that night, he was awakened by a violent storm. Water was breaking the ship and he heard the cry, "the ship is sinking!" The Captain issued an order to which John responded as the man who took his place on the ladder was washed overboard. Much later, he went to speak with the Captain as he was returning without much meaning, he is quoted as saying, "The Lord have mercy on us." This was his first plea for mercy. He had asked for many years and was instantly struck by his own words. Passages from the Bible came flooding back to him. He dreaded death. With every roll and toss of the ship, he felt that his last moment was imminent. He was on the pump for many hours until he was so utterly exhausted that he had to sleep. Within the hour he was awake and, too weak to man the pump, he took the helm.

He had plenty of time to contemplate. Hours later, when the ship was still afloat, John felt a glimmer of hope. Deeply conscious of his lack of faith, he began to pray.

The boat finally arrived in England. The girl he loved was still unattached. They married in 1750 and for the next few years, he was the Captain of a slave trade ship. He was deeply ashamed of this. Ill health prevented him from continuing his life at sea. He worked for a few years as a surveyor of tides in Liverpool. More and more he wanted to minister in the Church of England but was rejected. Sheer persistence brought reward. He was licensed as a Curate in Charge at Olney in 1764. In that same year his narrative was published; originally written as a collection of letters to a friend. Towards the end of his life, John became a little forgetful. He said, "Whatever else I forget, there are two things I shall remember; one, that I was a very great sinner; the second, that Christ is a very great Saviour." John Newton died in 1807.

BORN TO BE HUNTED

He is beautiful. He is bright

What a picture. What a sight!

His eyes gleam; he seems to smile

Not when the hounds chase him, many a mile

Just for fun; just for sport

I do hope, he isn't caught

He shouldn't kill the chickens though

He shouldn't be chased that way. No!

Blood sport is no good. It isn't fun

Especially if it's you they're making run.

Ban It! Ban it! That's what I cry

That's not fun, making foxes die.

Ramblings in literature - my favourite authors

When in an idle mood I enjoy visiting places where I have never been, I have many, my first Sicily with Etna smoking and then into the Lobo canyon both places from poetry by D. H Lawrence Snake and The Mountain Lion. These are my favourite works of Lawrence; I enjoy most of his short stories but consider his poetry contains his finest work. Many think it to be a by-product - some by-product more than 1200 poems! I have not found an author who gets nearer to nature. I find his stories of family pets, "Adolph" and "Rex" wonderful.

That is fantasy. I enjoy going back to moments of reality, times when I was touched with a nearness I cannot describe. Fighting the fire at Eastwood Church, Catherine's Shrine in York, Mansfield Crematorium and Saint Paul's Cathedral where my 8-year old son remarked "Dad, you wouldn't think man could make this" I believe my mother got this feeling when she visited the crypt in Saint Martin's in the Fields, London. She often spoke of those visits.

My favourite author is Steinbeck and my favourite prose is taken from Cannery Row. I quote, 'The Carmel is a lovely little river. It isn't very long but in its course it has everything a river should have. It rises in the mountains, and tumbles down a while, runs through shallows, is dammed to make a lake, spills over the dam, crackles among round boulders, wanders lazily under sycamores, spills into pools where trout live, drops in against banks where crayfish live. In winter it becomes a torrent, a mean little fierce river, and in the summer it is a place for children to wade in and for fishermen to wander in. Frogs blink from its banks and the deep ferns grow beside it. Deer and foxes come to drink from it, secretly in the morning and evening, and now and then a mountain lion crouched flat laps its water. The farms of the rich little valley back up to the river and take its water for the orchards and the vegetables. The quail calls beside it and the wild doves come whistling in at the dusk. Raccoons pace its edges looking for frogs. It's everything a river should be.'

So to another river the Irrawaddy, and the P.V. Pandau. She is the sole survivor of the flotilla of hundred or more of her sister ships that plied the Irrawaddy and scuppered in 1942 to deny the Japanese. The Pandau is a lovely ghost of her sunken sisters; she was built in Scotland 1947. She sails the Irrawaddy as if she owns it. This is by far the best way to get to Mandalay.

Despite what Kipling said, the road to Mandalay is dreadful; George Orwell thought the sharp irreverent spirit of Burma far better. Here is his poem

'When I was young in Mandalay, I gave my heart to a Burmese girl as lovely as the day, her skin was gold, her hair was jet, and her teeth were ivory. I said for twenty silver pieces, maiden sleep with me. She looked at me, so pure, so sad, the loveliest thing alive, and in her lisping voice, stood out for twenty five.' There is a good road out of Mandalay to the Chinese border, it's whispered to speed the traffic of Drugs, Guns and Laundered Money.

On to Oscar Wilde; I like his sayings, stories (including the ones for children), plays and poems. I find his poem, 'The Ballad of Reading Jail' very moving. He said he could resist anything but temptation. How life changes! So does the law! Wilde had the misfortune to have a homosexual relationship with the son of the 8th Marquess of Queensbury. For this he was sentenced to prison in Reading Jail for what now is lawful practice. I have the complete works of Wilde, with still much unread.

And so to Spike Milligan whose epitaph reads "I told you I was ill" - so much laughter united with manic depression. I think that to really know Spike, one must read "An intimate memoir" by Norma Farnes.

Neville Shute is another well-read author. Having read, 'A Town like Alice,' can one ever forget it? He worked alongside Barnes Wallace at Cardington, Bedfordshire. Cardington was where the R101 airship, along with others, was housed. I enjoyed 'Trustee from the Tool room' by Shute as well as much more of his work. Barnes Wallace born in Ripley, Derbyshire, went on to design the Wellington Bomber and the Bouncing Bomb for which he is famous. I know nothing of anything he has written.

The Long Walk by Slavomir Rawicz is a book I have enjoyed. Sometime after the Second World War he came to Sandiacre. He lived and died there. I never met him but did meet some of his relatives.

H.E. Bates is another writer I enjoy; he wrote well of nature just as D. H. Lawrence did. He was born in 1905 and died in 1973. He worked as a journalist until he was twenty, it was then he published his first book, The Two Sisters. He also wrote as 'Flying Officer X.' I believe he became known best when The Darling Buds of May was televised.

THE HOWITTS

William Howitt was born in Heanor Derbyshire on the 18th December 1792. His wife Mary Botham, a Quaker, was born in March 1799 at Coleford in Gloucester. Mary later resided temporarily in Uttoxeter, Staffs as her father was a prosperous Quaker in Uttoxeter.

She and William were married in 1821 at Hanley, Staffordshire and the marriage became a joint authorship with both being prolific writers. Mary started writing at an early age, being educated at home and had read a great deal; it was then she started writing verse. In 1837 she started writing her well-known tales for children, developing into a long and successful series of books.

William was educated at The Friends Public School Ackworth, Yorks. He was rather a precocious child, having his first work, "An Address to Spring," published when he was 13 years of age. His father wished for him to have a trade, so he became apprenticed to a builder in Mansfield. After getting his indentures, he returned to Heanor, working on his father's farm and also doing much study; learning French, Italian, chemistry, and botany along with the dispensing of medicine.

Soon after the wedding Mary wrote, 'after a summer and autumn in Hanley, my husband advantageous, disposed of his business. We moved to Heanor, where my parents in law had invited us to reside with them, until we could establish ourselves in Nottingham.' They lived in a house on Mansfield Road, near the junction of Hands Road. It projected well into the road, and I remember some of the wood from the demolitions being used for a Tithe Gate on Locton Avenue side entrance to the Heanor Cemetery: I now find it is in the Garden of Rest there.

It seems their Honeymoon was a walking tour of Scotland, then back to reality at Heanor. They then settled in Nottingham where William set up in business as a chemist. Both William and Mary were producing much literature. He produced the "Book of the Seasons" or "Calendar of Nature" and this ran to seven editions. His writing of "History of Priestcraft" involved him with the local Liberals and he was elected as an alderman. Finding that he was losing time on his greatest passion, writing, they moved to Esher, an outer suburb of London in 1836. In 1840 they moved into Heidelberg, mainly this was to better their sons' education. They had three sons, Alfred, William and Charlton. In 1852 it was with these three that he sailed to Australia to visit his brother, Dr Godfrey Howitt. This was also the only time William was separated from Mary during their marriage. It is recorded that he had practical experience of working in a gold mine while in Australia.

On returning to England in 1854 he wrote much on Australia. One of his works was "A History of Discovery in Australia." In "Poetry Please" first published in 1985, reprinted in 1994, 1995 (twice) we find "The Wind in a Frolic" – a poem that still gives me great pleasure.

From being Quakers they turned to Spiritualism, writing over a hundred articles for the Spiritual Magazine.

Starting in 1856 William wrote five volumes of "Popular History of England" he finished this in 1862; this work made seven editions.

The last years were spent in Rome. They both died of bronchitis – William on 3rd March 1879; Mary on 30th January 1888. I remember visiting Nottingham Castle when I was a small child and seeing the busts of William and Mary Howitt. On my last visit there in 2004 they were still on view. William's great-great grandfather was Thomas Howitt who, as a bachelor, resided in Eastwood Nottinghamshire. Thomas married Catherine Charlton of Chilwell, Nottinghamshire in 1680. I have read that this Thomas was a drunken gadabout and upset his father in law so much that Mr Charlton threatened his daughter that if she did not desert her husband, he would disown her. She would not leave him, so received none of her father's riches. During William's life the Charltons still thrived in Chilwell for William told of how his father, who was the manager of a coal mine, often entertained the joint owners of the mine namely, Squire Miller Mundy and Colonel Charlton at his home; this was while William was still a bachelor.

William's father was Thomas born in 1763, and it is said he brought a spirit of thrift, economy and sobriety back to the family. In 1786 he married Phoebe Tantum, the only daughter of Francis and Elizabeth Tantum who resided in The Fall, Midland Road, Heanor. The first Tantum I have read of was a Francis Tantum who was born in 1515 and was residing in Loscoe, Derbyshire and also the Tantums resided at The Fall for centuries. William had three elder brothers along with three younger brothers; I find no mention of sisters. The first-born was christened Tantum. Sadly he died in his fourth year. I find the Tantums exciting and interesting for Tantum Cottage was the second residence of my life, moving there in 1930. William was only three when his grandad Tantum died but he must have spoken, asked or even researched of him for he writes, 'at the period to which my mind runs back, my grandfather Tantum must have been near the close of his life. I was only in my third year when he died, yet I have a vivid recollection of him as a man of middle stature, but of substantial build, dressed in a dark Quaker suit and broad hat and with kind gentle manners. From my mother's account of his character, he was undecidedly of an intellectual turn and poetical taste, and I have no doubt that my brother Richard's literary idiosyncrasy, as well as my own, were derived from him. He occasionally wrote verses, but they were rather satirical squibs on the follies of some of his neighbours than any more ambitious attempts. His love of the best English writers was intense, and furnished him with the greatest enjoyment of his life, to me; it appears Milton was his favourite author.'

Mary Howitt wrote "My Uncle The Clock Maker" an interesting little book giving a vision of what life was like in the villages of Derbyshire was like in her time.

FA CUP 2006

On 27th April 2006, it was 60 years since Derby County won the FA Cup.

The Derby County eleven for the final tie was: -

- In goal - Vic Woodley (signed from Bath earlier in the season when he was not cup-tied) In the late thirties he was playing with Chelsea and at that time he was a regular choice for the England X1.

- Right back - and captain was Jack Nicholas. He was in his 18th year with the club. His father also played for Derby County.

- Left back - was Jack Howe. He had played in the semi-final replay replacing the injured Jack Parr. Howe had only been back in England three weeks after serving in the forces when he was called for the semi-final replay. He was selected to play in the final, replacing Jack Parr, who had played in all the other ties. Parr had broken his arm, so Howe played in the position he was later to fill for his country.

- The half back line - was Jim Bullions, Leon Leuty and Chick Musson. Leon Leuty was the centre half. Many of us thought he should have been in that England X1. I have never seen more elegance in a footballer in all my years of football and as I write I recapture it. What wonderful memories of a then marvellous game. Chick Musson was the left half. Both Chick and Jim were tenacious tacklers they also provided good distribution of the ball with head and feet.

- The centre forward was Jack Stamps, a burly strong man who would head anything that came his way! Remember this was the time of the leather ball with its leather lace. Jack paid for his courage and skill, for in much later days he would sit in the old Baseball Ground listening to the radio commentary through his earphones - yes, he had gone blind.

- The inside-forwards were Raich Carter and Peter Doherty. I am putting these two together for they were a perfect combination bringing out the best in each other. Their memory still lingers on. Raich was a silver haired maestro with a deadly shot. He schemed; he plotted and opened the defences with his passes. Peter was red headed; he was inventive; he would start attacks and finish them. He did things I had not seen done before, and some have never seen since.

Carter went on to become the manager of Hull City in 1948, taking them to promotion in quick time. Doherty also went into management. He took a third division team to promotion but he was soon to be lost to football.

- The wingers were: Dally Duncan, on the left. He was a Scottish international with wonderful ball control along with body swerve and good speed from a standing start. On the right was Reg Harrison, who by the injury to our famous winger Sammy Crooks, found himself in the daunting role of deputising for him. Sammy had been at Derby County longer than Jack Nicholas.

The FA cup competition of 1946 was different from all the others that preceded it. It was decided to have all rounds up to the semi-final played on the home away basis. This was the reason that Derby's opponents for the final, Charlton Athletic, were the first team to lose a match and play in the final. Derby got to the final by scoring 33 goals and conceding 7, in the 10 matches they played. The aggregate scores were Luton 9-0, West Brom Albion 4-1, Brighton 10-0, and in the 6th round 1st leg at Villa Park, witnessed by 76,588 spectators, a record for that ground, Derby won 4-3. This was the match in which Sammy Crooks received the injury, which caused him to miss the final. The second leg was a 1-1 draw. In the semi-final against Birmingham at Hillsborough the result was a 1-1 draw. The replay was at Maine Road, Manchester. A crowd of 80,407, a record for a mid-week match at that time; 90 minutes no score, so into extra time. Ted Duckhouse broke a leg; Doherty scored. Doherty was hailed and Duckhouse taken to the dressing room. Birmingham down to 10 men Derby scored 3 more and so to the final. This was the first post war final, in front of 98,215 spectators at Wembley. A great final, I am not going to relive it. Derby won 4-1 after extra time.

Burscough

Our journey to Burscough was uneventful, yet
beauty passed before our eyes.
We talked until the video. I put cotton wool in my
ears and lived with the changing scenes – Scenes
framed by the bus windows.
No artist could put on such a show.

Pheasants strutting, showing off – time for wooing
Then stark reality; deers contented, not knowing
that kindness brings an ulterior motive – dinner
plate.

Back to my vision - dreamy thoughts.
I remove my earplugs for a second but it's much too
loud! Effing and blinding – a film, Vinny Jones I
was told.
Now over the hills and dales
– a terrific place for hang-gliding. I wish I could
I can only fly kites now!

Hill - stream running down towards us
Soil - dried as though the tide's gone out.

Burscough, a village, I thought a town.
Railway station, a pub or two, shops,
Mills, no more producing,
A football team that beat us 2-0

The football ground on Bobby Langton Way
Happy memories of a fine left-winger, who played for England in his day.

ROBERT W. SERVICE

Robert Burns, born at Alloway, Ayrshire on 25th January 1759 is recognised as Scotland's most famous and National poet but their most commercially successful, is Robert Service

Robert Service is thought greatly of in Canada, where his life and work is one of the legends of the North West Territories. He was born on 16th January 1874 in Preston and has been hailed him as The Bard of The Yukon by the people of, the Yukon. He died a millionaire on 11th September 1958. His wealth had been mainly acquired from the writing of one poem namely, The Shooting of Dan McGrew. It became the biggest selling poem of all time, earning him at least five thousand dollars. His books of poetry sold millions of copies in his own lifetime and are still popular. His writings record a varied and full life, from clerk to cowboy, then from war correspondent to Hollywood celebrity. His publications also describe fascinating accounts of travel and adventures, which took him all over the world. He lived in Kilwinning with his grandparents for 5 years. When he celebrated his 6th birthday with them, they threw a party for him. At the party, he asked grandpa if he could say grace, telling him he had made one up. Grandpa said yes. Here is his first poem.

> God bless the cakes and bless the jam;
> Bless the cheese and cold boiled ham;
> Bless the scones Aunt Jeannie makes
> And save us all from belly aches. Amen.

This was immortalized in the old Post Office in Kilwinning on a plaque unveiled by his daughter Iris in 1976, which has now been repositioned on the wall in Main Street.

> A bunch of boys were whooping it up in the Malamute saloon.
>
> The kid that handled the music- box was hitting a jag time tune.
>
> Back of the bar, in a solo game, sat Dangerous Dan McGrew.
>
> And watching was his light-o-love, the lady that's known as Lou,
>
> When out of the night, which was fifty below, and into the din and the glare.
>
> Here stumbled a miner, fresh from the creeks, dog dirty and loaded for bear,
>
> He looked like a man with a foot in the grave, and scarcely the strength of a louse,

Yet he tilted a poke of dust on the bar, and he called for drinks for the house.

There was none could place the strangers face though we searched ourselves for a clue.

But we drank his health, and the last to drink was dangerous Dan McGrew.

He led a remarkable life, but was also a very private person and preferred not to write about his family and personal events, to the extent that even in his autobiographies people close to him would be referred to by fictitious names, with the dates and place names changed or omitted. However, thanks to diligent investigations of biographers such as Dr James MacKay we can begin to piece together Robert Service's remarkable story. In his autobiography he describes Kilwinning as the long Grey town. It is a North Ayrshire town, which traces it's history back nearly 1400 years to the coming of St Winnin, a medieval Abbey town built on the site of an early Celtic settlement. It is known as the cradle of Freemasonry because it has the Mother Lodge No.0; for being the place where President Eisenhower took his holidays, as well as for it's connections with Robert Service.

Service lived in Kilwinning for five years, watching his grandfather and aunts run their post office. He went to the local village school, and explored the town and surrounding countryside. Memories of his time in Kilwinning are captured in his rich descriptions of these early years.

Wanlockhead

BOXING

From my early days I have been interested in boxing and the first rules and regulations I ever read must have been in my father's encyclopaedia, his Internet of the 1930's, which defines boxing as follows: -
Boxing: Art of fighting with gloves on the fists. It is usually distinguished from prize fighting, or pugilism, in which no gloves are worn.

Pugilism is now illegal in Great Britain, but boxing is permitted by law, although in the case of death the principles and seconds are both liable to be tried for manslaughter. It then goes on to give the rules of The National Sporting Club London based on the rules drawn up by the 8th Marquess of Queensbury. I became involved with boxing at an early age and joined my first and only club in my teens. I am now to write about boxers I have admired, stories I have enjoyed and times I have been saddened.

One of the earliest fights I remember was when Joe Louis, the Brown Bomber beat Tommy Farr from Wales. It was 30th August 1937. I sat on the rug in front of the fire with my dad and brother. Ma was on the sofa. We listened to the fight, broadcast from New York for the Heavy Weight Championship of the World. We waited for the result eagerly and thought that Tommy had won, but no! Joe got the prize. Tommy was the second challenger for Joe's title. In all Joe had 27 fights to retain that title, losing the last one to Ezzard Charles on points over 15 rounds on 27th September 1950. Tommy Farr was one of only three challengers to go the distance with Joe.

Freddie Mills was born in Parkstone on 26th June 1919. Records show Bournemouth as the place of birth but a visit to Parkstone, will show that the people of this summer resort situated between Poole and Bournemouth take him as their son. He first put on boxing gloves when he was 13 years of age to spar with his brother Charlie who was a professional boxer at that time. Freddie said, "Many is the time I received clouts from mother for either getting a torn shirt or being covered in blood from these friendly bouts." His heart was set on boxing. On leaving school at 14 he started work as a milk boy being paid one pound per week. He was so keen on boxing he always carried a set of boxing gloves (that is 4 gloves) in his cycle bag, these came out most mornings between 8.00 and 9.00 am when he should have been breakfasting.

One and a half years later and seldom did a day or evening pass without him finding someone to spar with. He was feeling confident that he could swap punches with anyone. He spotted a Contest advert for 11 stone Novice Boxers. He got on his cycle and set off to put his name on the list - little did he know where this was going to take him. The competition gave him three fights. He won them all and was presented with a silver rose bowl. No one could have been more proud than Freddie, and he thought that was the end of his ring experience and glory for a while. He was wrong for the very next day the promoter called at his home asking him if he would like to box in a six round contest. He didn't have to ask again. The fight ended in a draw. His first professional fight earned him 18 shillings (90p) after expenses and he came out with about 10 bob (50p). He was now eager to learn the art of self-defence and enjoying swapping punches with anyone who would stand and swap them with him. He had another six- round fight, which also ended in a draw. He had now fought with boxers of some repute and decided to join a fairground-boxing booth. He was told of a booth in a fairground in Exeter and set off by bus from Bournemouth. The journey seemed to be endless but once in Exeter he quickly found the fairground and the boxing booth. As he approached the booth; a giant of a man was leaning on the pay kiosk. After contacting the proprietor and asking if he could join them Freddie was shown round and introduced to the giant of a man. It was no other than Gypsy Daniels whose real name was Billy. Gypsy had a cauliflower ear along with a broken nose. A few years earlier he had knocked out Max Schmeling and in the next two and a half months he was going to give Freddie a cauliflower ear and quite a few headaches. I find in the records that Gypsy Daniels was one of the busiest cruiserweights in the business. He was British Light heavy weight champion and relinquished his title in 1928. In that same year, he travelled to Germany and knocked out Schmeling who was the European Cruiserweight Champion. He did not claim the title. Freddie learnt the craft and with everyone but Billy he was the master. The show closed down in 3 months Freddie was saddened despite the thumps he had taken. He was able to join another travelling booth, namely Sam McKeown's Travelling Boxing Academy. He thought the academy would have some class men and he was right; he found that out to his discomfort! He was with the academy for nearly 3 years, boxing daily and often to the early hours of the next day. Running behind the caravan on the travels was his roadwork, he became super fit as the erecting and dismantling of the show built up his strength. Sometimes he would face as many as twelve opponents in a day then crawl under the ring to his bed still with the bandages on his hands, and wearing his shorts and dressing gown. He became a professional boxer while with the academy, fighting in licensed halls as well as in the booth. By the time he was twenty he had 55 contests that were in the records.

Freddie related a couple of lighter things that happened in the academy. The first, a certain coloured gentleman was sleeping under the ring. Freddie went to tell him that he was next on, adding, "watch his right cross, it's deadly!" They picked him up only seconds after that first bell, then put him back under the ring to sleep it off. Sometime later asking how the gentleman felt Freddie got the reply, "When I woke up I'd had a terrible dream!" That unfortunate gentleman would never accept he had been knocked out.

The other tale was about a woman visiting the academy to sort out the bloke who had beat her husband up. She chased the boy round the fairground. He got away and stayed in the caravan till the next day! The academy closed with the outbreak of war. In January 1940 Freddie joined the R.A.F. and before long he was sent on exhibitions entertaining the services and raising money for charities etc. On the 20th June 1942 he became the British and Commonwealth Light Heavy Champion by knocking out Len Harvey in the 2nd round of the title fight at White Hart Lane, London. He retained this title until he retired from the ring in 1950. He was the undefeated Light Heavy Weight Champion of Europe from 1947 to 1950.

World Light Heavy Weight Champion (GB Version) from 1942 to 1946. In 1946 he fought Gus Lesnevich the American version of world champion, who beat him after a great fight. Two years later they met again. Mills won this contest on points to become the undisputed Light Weight Champion of the World.

He lost the title in 1950 to the American Joey Maxim. In his professional career from 1936 to 1950, Freddie Mills had 101 contests, won 77, drew 6 and lost 18. He retired from the ring immediately becoming a TV personality and appeared in films. Later he was involved with the nightlife of London and became owner of a nightclub. In 1965 he was found shot dead in his car.

Stanley Park

I'd been to the coffee morning at the Cricket Club.
I met Steven Kennedy; we climbed the steps together.
I met Beryl who introduced me to 3 fellow members. I related the tale of Tiger, the cricket club cat.

Tiger acquired his name by his appearance but he lived up to it by his actions. He didn't mind being stroked sometimes but when he'd had enough, he'd bite the hand that was stroking him. He didn't like being picked up but Tom, the groundsman's assistant always tried to pick him up and consequently got bit most days, always stating "that bloody cat's wild." Howard, the groundsman, always told him, "Don't try to pick him up, then!" It was the same every day.

Tiger lived in the boiler house. There was one small window frame with no glass, which was his entrance and also where he spent a good deal of his time. Through the boiler house and into the room, adjacent to which was the grounds man's workshop. Tiger would come in here when anyone was having a snack. Although the times varied, he knew when food and refreshment was being taken by the sound of the sandwich tins being opened and mugs clattering onto the bench.

One day Tom came running to Howard. "Tiger's nearly dead! He's lying in the grass over there!" Howard went over. "You're right. I'll take him to the vet" and proceeded to do so. The vet said, "He's in a bad way. There's just a chance with some tablets I've got." The vet gave Tiger one tablet and told Howard to give him about 3 a day. On arrival back at the cricket ground, Howard put Tiger in a basket, leaving him in a corner of the boiler house, then got on with his work. After about half an hour of mowing, he looked up on the top of the pavilion. Tiger was doing his usual patrol; actually crouching, ready to pounce on an unsuspecting bird. Howard thought, "My! Those tablets are good!" A few hours later, Howard returned to the boiler house. Tiger ran to him and waited. Then behind him, with his tail straight up, looking realistically into the boiler house. All hell broke loose – a sick ringer of Tiger in his place! Double trouble!! Tiger number two!

Another Close Call

On 27th September 2006 many thoughts passed through my head within seconds. I had spoken with David, made an appointment with the doctor, was taking my first spoonful of breakfast, I had porridge oats with pineapple. I tasted the juice, my throat contracted, I was unable to take in breath stumbled to the floor pushed the red alarm button, still gasping waiting for an answer, and trying to open my throat for an airway, I got the answer and tried to tell my predicament. Fortunately my neighbours had heard me and came through my flat door, which was unlocked, to my rescue. By the time the paramedics arrived I had recovered. They did tests and gave me the all clear. I saw Dr. Ashworth later in the morning she thought it was a panic attack that caused the problem. I said the only panic was after the attack, I thought my time was up. I have faced death a few times most of them while unconscious, seventeen years ago I did not think I wanted to live but found I did, I thank God. I am enjoying life and so thankful.

ASS U ME

What makes an ass of you and me?

To assume, you will agree.

Think positive, work it out,

Reach a logical solution

Take nothing for granted.

Listen to reason

Learn by others' mistakes

Life becomes easier

The way becomes clear

Barriers fall down

No need to fight

Keep that perfect ending ever in sight.

I live to love

I live to love
My love is free
I don't make love
Love makes me

My love grows
and will always be
I don't make love
Love makes me.

I am a fool
that's what they say
I am what I am
But this I know.
Without love,
I've nowhere to go.

To my grandchildren – Rebecca & Julie

I love you more than words can say
I love you more and more each day
I love you both 'til I can love no more
My love will stay with you forevermore.

Yet I love Jesus, so why cannot I do all that He wants me to.
It's because I find comfort in my sadness but there is joy too,
For through Jesus, nearness to all I love will never leave me.

Don's Sayings

"I don't assume, I just take what I get from you"

"You don't know how bloody lucky you are."

"Am tip top."

Memories of the Heanor boy...
"Mrs Parkin saw me brought into this world and here I am, seeing her out."

It's better now than when it was worse than what it is.

You wouldn't have me any other way, would you?

If I walk out that door and never come back again, you will not forget me.

That's all folks – from Donald